Writing Common Criteria Documentation

Writing Common Criteria Documentation

Wesley Hisao Higaki

Writing Common Criteria Documentation

ISBN-13:
978-1500411220

ISBN-10:
1500411221

Acknowledgments

I give my warmest thanks to my friends and family, especially to my wife, Naomi, for supporting me in everything I do.

Special thanks to my daughter, Yukie, for designing the cover of this book.

I especially want to thank my good friend, Ray Potter for giving me the chance to contribute to his consulting business and enabling me to gain the experience I've needed to write this book.

I have a special acknowledgment for Henry Hernandez and my friends at CyberSecurity Malaysia for inspiring me to tackle this topic.

About the Author

Wes Higaki led the product certification program at Symantec Corporation for seven years. He set the product security certification strategy and managed all of the certification projects. In that role, Wes reviewed and edited the documentation used in the evaluations. Wes wrote *Successful Common Criteria Evaluations: A Practical Guide for Vendors* in 2010 to help others by sharing his insights into the Common Criteria process.

Wes has contributed to the public awareness of the Common Criteria by co-founding the Common Criteria Vendors' Forum (CCVF). The CCVF was an informal group of representatives from commercial product companies that were actively involved in Common Criteria evaluation to discuss issues and to serve as the "voice of industry" in the Common Criteria global community.

Most recently, Wes has been a Common Criteria consultant creating Common Criteria documentation and providing project management for product developers.

Wes has over 30 years of technical and managerial experience in the software industry. He has held management positions at Symantec, Axent Technologies, and over 20 years at Hewlett-Packard Company.

Wes received a Bachelor of Science degree in mathematics from the University of California, Davis and a Master of Science degree in computer science from Santa Clara University.

Connect with Wes through LinkedIn.com at:
www.linkedin.com/in/weshigaki

Table of Contents

Table of Figures

Table of Tables

PART I: BACKGROUND

This part contains:

Chapter 1: Introduction

The Common Criteria for Information Technology Security Evaluation (or the Common Criteria) is an internationally recognized (as ISO 15408) standard for the declaration of security functional claims in information technology (IT) products and the independent validation of those claims through the examination of evidence (documentation) and product testing.

The purpose of this book is to provide guidance to those interested in producing the documentation required for successfully completing a Common Criteria (CC) commercial product security evaluation.

CC documentation requirements are defined by the CC Part 3 and the assessment requirements are defined in the Common Evaluation Methodology (CEM) standards. This book is based on the Common Criteria version 3.1 revision 4 standards. The specific documentation requirements are driven by the Evaluation Assurance Level (EAL) selected by the developer. This book will cover the specific requirements for EAL2 and EAL4 because in my experience, the most common EALs used by commercial product developers are EAL2 and EAL4.

Motivation for this Book

I have been involved in CC evaluations since 2002 where I oversaw the EAL4 evaluation of a Symantec firewall product using a UK evaluation lab. I have since been involved in the evaluation of dozens of products. Over the years, I have played many roles in the process. At Symantec I acted as the corporate coordinator for all CC evaluations for the company. I also was deeply involved in the review and development of the CC documentation used in the evaluations. I provided strategic and tactical guidance on the approach to CC evaluations.

Most recently, I have been a consultant with Apex Assurance Group developing CC documentation for product vendors. Through these varied consulting engagements, I have had the opportunity to work with a wide variety of product technologies, development processes, and testing approaches. I have also gained experience working with labs and Schemes from the UK, Canada, Australia, Sweden, Norway, and the US.

Using this breadth and depth of experience, I have developed an approach that has enabled me to create the documentation necessary to successfully complete dozens of EAL1 through EAL4 evaluations.

Recently, I have been approached by clients to provide training for their staff members to produce their own CC documents. As I exit the CC consultant profession, I thought I'd collect my thoughts and experiences in this book to provide some guidance to these clients and others who would like to learn how to write their own CC documents or perhaps be able to assess the quality of CC documents produced by others. My hope is that with these insights that developers can create CC documents that make the evaluation process go more quickly, smoothly, and cost-effectively.

How this Book Is Organized

Part I of this book provides the background and motivation for writing this book. It also includes an overview of the CC documentation requirements for EAL2 and EAL4. I also share some of my thoughts on how to conduct an effective CC evaluation project.

Part II covers the requirements for the Security Target document, the foundational document for all CC evaluations. I have also provided some tips on defining the scope of the evaluation.

Part III describes the requirements for each Lifecycle document required for EAL2 and EAL4. The documents covered are: Configuration Management, Delivery, Lifecycle Support, and Development Security. Flaw Remediation is a commonly used augmentation of EAL2 and EAL4, so these document requirements are also covered in Part III. I have also included a chapter covering the site visit.

Part IV of this book details the requirements for the Development documents. The documentation requirements vary greatly between EAL2 and EAL4. This part covers the requirements for Security Architecture, Functional Specifications, Basic Design, Basic Modular Design, and Implementation Representation.

Part V explains the Guidance requirements. The Operational User Guidance and Preparative Procedures Guidance document is intended to augment the standard product documentation but provides evaluation-specific instructions for evaluators.

Part VI covers the test documentation and testing requirements. The Test Plan is the main CC document that supports developer and lab testing.

Part VII provides closing remarks and reference materials for this book.

In each chapter I include the relevant requirements directly from the CC standards as reference. I explain what the requirements mean in terms of the content required in the documentation. I provide some insights into what the evaluator will do with the information provided in the documentation. I follow this up with templates and examples.

Disclaimer and Warning

This book is written in the spirit of my first book *Successful Common Criteria Evaluations: A Practical Guide for Vendors* [Higaki] in that my intended audience is product developers interested in successfully completing Common Criteria evaluations for their commercial products. My working assumption is that these product vendors merely want to get through the evaluation and certification process so that they can satisfy a procurement requirement. With that in mind, *Writing Common Criteria Documentation* presents material so that the reader can be as effective and efficient as they can toward completing the CC evaluation.

My warning to the reader is that even though this book attempts to capture what I have learned over my 12 years of experience with several different CC Schemes, labs, and evaluators, there are no guarantees that I have covered all of the possible situations and scenarios that can emerge during an evaluation. I have found that in spite of the fact that there exists a fairly detailed documented international standard, there is still quite a bit of interpretation imposed by the certifiers and evaluators. There are no hard-and-fast rules in CC evaluations.

I have also found a wide variation in the level of technical understanding of product technologies amongst certifiers and evaluators. While this book provides more details about the documentation requirements in the CC standards, I have found that depending on the level of experience or technical knowledge of the certifiers and evaluators there may be a need to provide more detail in the CC documentation in order to explain how things work.

My experience has shown that it takes a certain mental approach to developing successful CC documentation. Since you have to develop documentation and provide explanations to satisfy evaluators and certifiers, it becomes important to understand their objectives, motivations, and constraints. I have tried to impart some of those notions throughout this book but there are no guarantees that these methods will work in all instances.

As I pointed out in Chapter 3: Process Overview of my book *Successful Common Criteria Evaluations: A Practical Guide for Vendors* [Higaki], evidence rework is a significant effort in the CC evaluation process. While the guidance I provide in this book helps prepare the necessary documentation, the role of the evaluator is to comment on the evidence documents and apply his/her judgment on how well that evidence meets the requirements according to the instructions they are given. Their comments must be addressed either through updates to the documentation or through explanations to the evaluator. It is the iteration of these comment-and-response cycles that extends the time it takes to complete the evaluation.

Finally, please note that throughout this book I quote sections from the CC standards which use British English spellings such as "initialisation" and "behaviour." There are also apparent grammatical errors in the standards. In order to retain the integrity of these citations, I've copied the spellings and any potential grammar errors directly from these references to avoid possible misinterpretations on my part.

Chapter 2: Assurance Requirements

The CC assurance documentation requirements are defined in the CC Part 3 [CC3] and the Common Evaluation Methodology (CEM). CC Part 3 provides the requirements for the developer, contents of the assurance documents, and some instructions for the evaluators. The [CEM] provides more detailed instructions for the evaluator that can lend insights into what specific requirements need to be met in the CC documentation.

CC Part 3 Assurance Documentation Requirements

CC assumes that assurance is derived from the examination of vendor evidence by independent, accredited laboratories. This evidence comes primarily from documentation from the developer (and/or their contracted consultants). CC Part 3 provides the documentation requirements through **developer action elements** and **content and presentation elements** of each assurance class and family. An example of a requirement in CC Part 3 is:

AGD_OPE.1 Operational user guidance

Developer action elements:
AGD_OPE.1.1D The developer shall provide operational user guidance.

Content and presentation elements:
AGD_OPE.1.1C The operational user guidance shall describe, for each user role, the user-accessible functions and privileges that should be controlled in a secure processing environment, including appropriate warnings....

The assurance class in the example is denoted AGD for Assurance – Guidance. The assurance family within the AGD class is OPE for operational user guidance. The number 1.1 denotes the component and subcomponent. The developer action element describes the high-level requirement for the developer. The content and presentation elements provide greater details for the developer action element. There are typically several content and presentation elements for each developer action element.

The individual CC documents typically address one class of assurance requirements. In our example, there will be one document created to address the guidance (AGD class) assurance requirements.

The detailed documentation requirements as presented in [CC3] vary depending on the Evaluation Assurance Level (EAL) selected by the developer. The following tables summarize the EAL2 assurance requirements.

ASSURANCE CLASS	COMPONENTS
ASE: Security Target	ASE_INT.1 ST introduction
	ASE_CCL.1 Conformance claims
	ASE_SPD.1 Security problem definition
	ASE_OBJ.2 Security objectives
	ASE_ECD.1 Extended components definition
	ASE_REQ.2 Derived security requirements
	ASE_TSS.1 TOE summary specification
ALC: Life-cycle support	ALC_CMC.2 Use of a CM system
	ALC_CMS.2 Parts of the TOE CM coverage
	ALC_DEL.1 Delivery procedures
ADV: Development	ADV_ARC.1 Security architecture description
	ADV_FSP.2 Security-enforcing functional specification
	ADV_TDS.1 Basic design
AGD: Guidance	AGD_OPE.1 Operational user guidance
	AGD_PRE.1 Preparative procedures
ATE: Tests	ATE_COV.1 Evidence of coverage
	ATE_FUN.1 Functional testing
	ATE_IND.2 Independent testing - sample
AVA: Vulnerability assessment	AVA_VAN.2 Vulnerability analysis

Table 1 - EAL2 Assurance Requirements

The table below lists the assurance requirements for EAL4.

ASSURANCE CLASS	COMPONENTS
ASE: Security Target	ASE_INT.1 ST introduction
	ASE_CCL.1 Conformance claims
	ASE_SPD.1 Security problem definition
	ASE_OBJ.2 Security objectives
	ASE_ECD.1 Extended components definition
	ASE_REQ.2 Derived security requirements
	ASE_TSS.1 TOE summary specification
ALC: Life-cycle support	ALC_CMC.4 Production support, acceptance procedures and automation
	ALC_CMS.4 Problem tracking CM coverage
	ALC_DEL.1 Delivery procedures
	ALC_DVS.1 Identification of security measures
	ALC_LCD.1 Developer defined life-cycle model
	ALC_TAT.1 Well-defined development tools
ADV: Development	ADV_ARC.1 Security architecture description
	ADV_FSP.4 Complete functional specification
	ADV_IMP.1 Implementation representation of the TSF
	ADV_TDS.3 Basic modular design
AGD: Guidance	AGD_OPE.1 Operational user guidance
	AGD_PRE.1 Preparative procedures
ATE: Tests	ATE_COV.2 Analysis of coverage
	ATE_DPT.1 Testing: basic design
	ATE_FUN.1 Functional testing
	ATE_IND.2 Independent testing - sample
AVA: Vulnerability assessment	AVA_VAN.3 Focused vulnerability analysis

Table 2 - EAL4 Assurance Requirements

In this book I will explain each requirement and describe how each requirement can be met through documentation. Chapters in this book will highlight and explain what documents and content is required for EAL2 and EAL4.

In addition, I will explain the requirements for Flaw Remediation (ALC_FLR.1 and ALC_FLR.2) as commercial developers commonly use this "augmentation" of the standard EAL2 and EAL4 packages to explain their defect management processes.

Common Evaluation Methodology

I have found that it is not sufficient to simply address assurance requirements in [CC3] in the CC documents in order to successfully complete the evaluation. Evaluators are given specific instructions on what to evaluate and to a degree, how to evaluate the CC documentation. These instructions are provided in the Common Evaluation Methodology [CEM]. In some cases, the CEM requires the evaluator to evaluate items that were not explicitly stated as requirements in [CC3]. Also, the evaluator is allowed to use their own judgment and interpretations in their evaluation efforts. In this book, I include the assurance requirements for developer action, content, and presentation elements directly from the CC standards [CC3]. I also provide an interpretation based on my experience for what the requirements actually mean and how to sufficiently address the requirements. I also provide insights into what the evaluator must do to satisfy the requirements within [CEM] (although I do not provide the actual descriptions from CEM in this book) and how that affects the content and presentation of the CC documents.

Chapter 3: Documentation Tips

I did not intend this book to describe the details of the CC evaluation process as I did in *Successful Common Criteria Evaluations: A Practical Guide for Vendors* [Higaki] but I wanted to share here a few tips based on my experiences with many CC evaluation projects that I think can help reduce the time and effort involved in producing CC documentation evidence towards a successful CC evaluation project.

Manage the project scope

In Chapter 4: Preparation for the ST, I provide tips on how to appropriately set the Target of Evaluation (TOE) Boundary to reduce project risk. The TOE Boundary and the Security Target set the foundation for the entire evaluation project. The CC evaluation should be treated like any other project using sound project management practices with consideration for return-on-investment (ROI), cost and resource constraints, deadlines, and customer satisfaction. Setting clear project objectives at the beginning of the project will help to guide the decision-making process throughout the project. My goal has always been to successfully complete the CC evaluation on budget.

The TOE is a snapshot in time

Remember that the TOE is a "snapshot in time" of the product. Commercial products get updated periodically for bug fixes and upgrades. The specific version of the product that will be the final TOE may be a moving target if the evaluation takes longer than expected. Any modification of the TOE during the evaluation will result in some form of documentation update (at a minimum the TOE Reference will change) and delays in completing the evaluation. The final version of the TOE must be available when the lab performs their independent testing.

Do not modify documents unnecessarily

Once the initial version of any CC evidence document has been sent to the evaluation lab, it is a good idea to be judicious about making

25

changes to those documents unless they are in response to comments from the lab or the government certifiers. There is a temptation to try to be more technically accurate or to include additional detail to the documents even though the evaluators did not ask for it. Resist this temptation. Oftentimes, such embellishment leads to more questions from the evaluators and more work for you.

Double-check for consistency across documents

A high percentage of the comments from evaluators are due to inconsistencies they find between documents. As a quality control check before submitting a document to the lab, it is a good idea to review it for consistency with the other documents that the lab has already reviewed. For example, the server portion of the TOE may be called "XYZ Service" in the Security Target (ST) but the label "XYZ Server" is used in the Security Architecture (ARC) document. This will be flagged immediately by the evaluator and an update to either the ST or ARC will be expected. Also, inconsistencies in the labels used in illustrations and diagrams are common errors.

Recognize the importance of resource commitment

In my experience, the single greatest risk to CC projects is the lack of commitment from key resources. Technical subject matter experts (SME) are required to provide detailed internal product design information. They are also needed to review documentation for accuracy. They are also probably the busiest people in the organization. Lack of priority given to the CC project will certainly doom or significantly delay it.

Provide timely response to lab and certifier comments

The fallout of the lack of resource commitment is delayed responses to comments from the lab. These delays will throw off the lab's evaluation work plan and possibly put the project in jeopardy of violating some of the government certifier's deadlines. This could result in getting kicked off the "in evaluation" list and possibly affect the ability to sell the product to customers.

Make it easier for the evaluator to do their job

[CC3] and [CEM] dictate what the evaluator must do to evaluate the CC documentation from the developer. For example, the ST's TOE Summary Specifications (TSS) must explain how each Security Functional Requirement (SFR) is met by the TOE. The evaluator will have an easier time figuring out which paragraph in the TSS relates to which SFR if the SFR identifier (e.g., FAU_GEN.1, FDP_IFC.1) is noted in the relevant text of the TSS. In the following chapters, I suggest different ways to present the necessary information to the evaluators in an efficient manner.

Evaluators provide comments on the documents. Developers provide updates to respond to those comments. Microsoft Word and other word processing programs have a "change tracking" feature that can make it easier for the evaluator to find the specific changes made in response to their comments. This saves time and money.

Reduce document rework

Document rework is a fact of life with CC document evaluations and is the greatest threat to successfully completing CC evaluations on-time and on-budget. Avoiding rework requires focus on the objectives of the project, understanding the requirements, and understanding the expectations of the evaluators. The following chapters in this book aim to provide some insights into how that can be accomplished.

Some evaluation labs charge developers a "fixed price" for their evaluation effort. Be aware that these "fixed price" arrangements may actually only be fixed price for a limited number of rework cycles. I was once unpleasantly surprised to find out that a contract I had with a lab was "fixed price plus" meaning we could go through 2 rework cycles on any given document before being charged on an hourly basis. This is another reason to try to reduce documentation rework.

Document Evaluation Process

Most CC evaluation projects follow the same sequence of document development and review. The following diagram illustrates the typical flow of the development of the CC evidence documents. Most evaluation labs and their national Schemes allow for incremental submittal and evaluation of the CC evidence documentation. Only in rare instances have I encountered the requirement to deliver the entire documentation package (i.e., Security Target, Lifecycle Support, Development, Guidance, and Test) simultaneously.

The Security Target (ST) is the first document that has to be produced and evaluated. It is the foundational piece of the evaluation. It defines the scope of the evaluation and sets the stage for all of the rest of the documentation and evaluation effort. Once the ST has been developed, it is usually convenient to begin the development of the Lifecycle Support (ALC) documents that describe the developer's configuration management, delivery, and other secure development practices because these are process-oriented documents and are fairly independent of the other documents.

The Development (ADV) documents that describe the internal designs of the target product usually take time to produce so this effort should be started as soon as the scope of the evaluation has been determined. The Guidance (AGD) documents provide instructions on how to install, configure, and use the product in the "evaluated configuration." These instructions are used by the evaluation lab during their independent testing phase and should be provided prior to their testing. The Test Plan (ATE) document records the test procedures and results obtained by the developer to prove that the security functionality performs as claimed in the ST. The evaluation lab will verify the test results and conduct their own testing using the ATE and AGD documents to guide them.

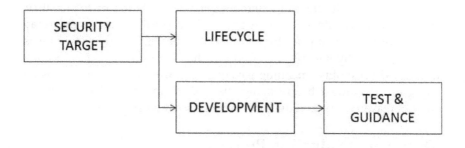

Figure 1 - Document Development Phases

Responding to Evaluator Comments

For each document that is written by the developer, it is re-viewed (evaluated) by the contracted Common Criteria Testing Labora-tory (CCTL). The evaluators will evaluate each document using instruc-instructions from the CC standards [CC3] and [CEM] as well as guidance from their national Scheme. The developer will receive comments from the lab and is expected to provide a response to correct any issues or address any questions. This cycle is often called evidence rework. The evaluator and developer will cycle through until all of the issues have been resolved satisfactorily and the document passes. The diagram below shows this cycle.

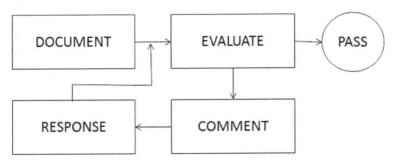

Figure 2 - Document Rework Cycle

The comments from the evaluators are formally called Evalua-tion Observation Reports (EORs). These reports tend to serve multiple purposes: recording the observations/comments from the evaluators for the lab's internal tracking; reporting results to the certifiers; and provid-ing inputs to the developer on the deficiencies/errors in the documents. The format and detailed content of these reports to the developer vary widely between evaluation labs because they serve these multiple purposes. The comments within these reports range from specific and helpful to general and non-helpful for the developer.

I have received comments from evaluators that clearly defined the deficiency or error in the document. Some comments even provided suggestions on how to correct the document. For example, I've received comments such as the following.

The TSS description of how the TOE meets FAU_GEN.1.1a is missing the description of how the TOE logs the start-up and shutdown of the audit functions. Please explain which logs are used to record these events.

I have also received much less helpful comments such as the one below.

The FSP lacks the level of detail necessary to satisfy ADV_FSP.2.1C. The functional specification shall completely represent the TSF.

Most evaluators welcome questions from the developers when their comments are not clear enough to provide a satisfactory response. I strongly recommend that if the comments are not clear that the developer schedule a conference call with the evaluator to gain a better understanding for what the evaluator is saying and what kind of response would be satisfactory. Too often, miscommunication causes unnecessary rework cycles and delays in the project.

PART II: SECURITY TARGET

This part contains::

Chapter 4:   Preparation for the ST

Typically, developers of commercial products faced with embarking on a CC evaluation already have a product and they need to evaluate an existing (shipping) version of the product or a version that is due to be released in the near future. I have never encountered the situation where a developer is creating a commercial product from scratch and is deciding on how to meet the requirements for a CC evaluation. These typical situations mean that the developer and ST author need to define the scope of the evaluation and the TOE Boundary based on the features that exist in the target product. This chapter discusses an effective method for accomplishing this.

ST Creation Process

I prefer to start creating the Security Target (ST) by creating the TOE Summary Specifications (TSS) first. The TSS is a prosaic explanation of how the TOE meets the claimed security functions. The TSS is the last section of the ST so it may seem like this process is backward from what it should be. Because most evaluations are for existing products, I have found it is easier to write the ST by first determining what CC security-relevant functions the product already has, describing them in prose, translating them into CC language, and finally creating the Security Problem Definition.

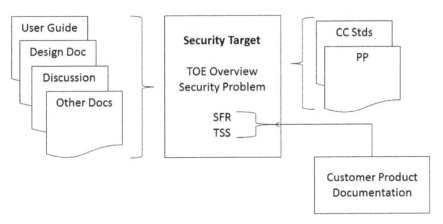

Figure 3 - ST Creation Process

As illustrated in the figure above, the material I use to write the TSS includes customer product documentation, internal design documentation, and discussions with product experts. By reviewing these materials and drawing upon my own experience with similar products and technologies as well as an understanding of CC relevant security functions, I am able to create a description of the eligible product security functions. This description goes into the TSS as well as the TOE Overview.

As I go through the product reference material (especially product manuals), I annotate the sections that represent security functions I include in the TSS so that when I need more details about the functions, I can readily find the appropriate information. This is particularly handy when it is time to write the Functional Specifications (FSP) which requires more of these details.

Next, I develop the Security Requirements section of the ST by translating the security functions from the TSS into standard Security Functional Requirements (SFRs). I use the CC Standards documents [CC2] as a catalog of potential security claims. I explain how to do this later in this chapter. If the evaluation claims conformance to a Protection Profile (PP), the PP will dictate the specific functional claims. See the section About Protection Profiles later in this chapter for more details.

TOE Boundary

The Security Target (ST) document is the foundation of the CC evaluation. It defines what is going to be evaluated called the TOE Boundary. The TOE Boundary defines what features of the commercial product will be included in the evaluation. For example, a network router is delivered to customers in a hardware box provided by the developer along with pre-loaded firmware and software. This box contains proprietary chips and circuitry that perform specialized functions. The TOE in this case probably will be the entire appliance with a specific version of the firmware and software. The trick to defining a good TOE Boundary is to clearly identify what are the relevant security features for the CC evaluation.

Common Criteria allegedly is an evaluation of security features of a designated TOE. However, the definition of security features in the context of CC is oftentimes different from what developers typically think it is. At one level, developers think about security in terms of preventing the introduction of product defects that could be vulnerabilities. They also think about security features such as encrypting user data in transit or inspecting network packets for possible attacks. They will rarely think of audit logging or system configuration as security features although these are features covered by CC. Defining what product features should be covered in the CC evaluation is the key question in defining the TOE Boundary and writing an effective, practical Security Target.

Most developers just want to get a CC certificate as quickly, easily, painlessly, and cost-effectively as possible. Given this as the objective, defining an appropriate TOE Boundary is critical. In this chapter, I share some of my thoughts on how to properly scope the evaluation and define the TOE Boundary in preparation for writing the Security Target.

The focus of my advice deals primarily with security feature claims. The tips fall into the following categories:

- Use CC Standard Security Features
- Minimize TOE Scope
- Minimize System Configurations

Use CC Standard Security Features

The CC community has invested millions of person-hours and millions of dollars to develop the CC standards. CC Part 2 [CC2] has been developed by security experts to cover a wide range of IT products and the breadth of generic security functions. The CC standards [CC1], [CC2], [CC3], and [CEM] are an integrated package of requirements and instructions that aim to smooth the evaluation process. Using the standard Security Functional Requirements (SFRs) as defined in [CC2] wherever practical will help eliminate friction in the evaluation process.

I am not a fan of the use of Extended Components in Security Functional Requirement (SFR) claims. The CC standards [CC1] allow for the creation and definition of customized or extended security functional requirements in Section 5 of the Security Target. Some developers view this capability as an opportunity to showcase some unique feature of their product. I advocate not using this capability because creating extended SFRs introduces the opportunity for evaluators and certifiers to use non-standard means to evaluate the function which may lead to a more difficult testing phase.

Selecting security functions from an existing product that properly match the SFRs in [CC2] does require some expertise and understanding of the CC standards. Here I will provide some insights into some of the more "popular" SFRs and how to interpret them and the implications of using them. I will provide additional details in the section of Chapter 5: Security Target discussing the Security Requirements section of the ST.

CC standard SFRs are collected and organized into Security Functional Classes (SFC). There are a total of 11 SFCs defined by [CC2]. In this book, I've selected the most popular SFRs based on my experience and review of Security Targets from other commercial products. I believe that the reason these SFRs are commonly used is because they are practical and most easily applicable to commercial products.

The SFCs I will cover in this chapter and their identifiers are:
- Security Audit (FAU)
- Cryptographic Support (FCS)
- User Data Protection (FDP)
- Identification and Authentication (FIA)
- Security Management (FMT)
- Protection of the TOE Security Function (FPT)
- Trusted Path/Channels (FTP)

Please note that the CC standards often refer to the TOE Security Functions (TSF). It is defined as the "combined functionality of all hardware, software, and firmware of a TOE that must be relied upon for the correct enforcement of the SFRs." For the purposes of this book, the terms TOE and TSF are synonymous.

Selecting SFRs to include in the ST from the standard set in [CC2] go beyond just identifying the security functions the TOE supports. Many SFRs have dependencies; that is, in order to claim support for one SFR, the TOE must also meet all of the dependencies defined by the CC standard. For example, the FDP_ITT.1 Basic internal transfer protection SFR has the following requirements:

FDP_ITT.1 Basic internal transfer protection

Management: FDP_ITT.1
The following actions could be considered for the management functions in FMT:
a) If the TSF provides multiple methods to protect user data during transmission between physically separated parts of the TOE, the TSF could provide a pre-defined role with the ability to select the method that will be used.

Audit: FDP_ITT.1
The following actions should be auditable if FAU_GEN Security audit data generation is included in the PP/ST:

a) Minimal: Successful transfers of user data, including identification of the protection method used.
b) Basic: All attempts to transfer user data, including the protection method used and any errors that occurred.

Dependencies:
[FDP_ACC.1 Subset access control, or
FDP_IFC.1 Subset information flow control]

The Management requirement in the example states that an SFR in the Security Management (FMT) class should be included in the ST to describe the capability to select the method used to protect data transmitted between separate parts of the TOE (e.g., client to server.)

The Audit requirement in the example illustrates that if FAU_GEN.1 is claimed then the TOE should audit the data transfer events between the separate parts of the TOE. See my comments about the complications of FAU_GEN.1 later in this chapter.

The Dependencies requirement indicates an SFR is not self-sufficient and relies upon the functionality of, or interaction with, another SFR for its own proper functioning. These dependency SFRs must be included in the ST along with the initial SFR.

This example illustrates how a single SFR may require other SFRs to be included in the ST and the requirements for each need to be met by the TOE. If it is determined that the TOE does not completely meet all of these requirements, the initial SFR may need to be eliminated from the scope of the evaluation. This illustrates how care must be taken when selecting SFRs for consideration for inclusion in the ST.

Security Audit (FAU)

Computer forensics is an important security tool. Being able to look back into the history of security-related events helps address vulnerabilities and attack methods. The Security Audit class of SFRs is the way CC attempts to capture these security features.

The two most popular and widely claimed Security Audit SFRs are FAU_GEN.1 Audit data generation and FAU_SAR.1 Audit review for products that log security events. These two SFRs are very generic and can easily be applied to many commercial products. The other SFRs in the FAU class are more specialized and have to be reviewed carefully against the product (TOE) actual specific capabilities. For example the FAU_SEL.1 Selective audit functions allow users to select which events

37

to include or exclude from auditing based on certain criteria. I've found that this SFR may be most applicable to intrusion detection systems where security event logs can be "noisy" without proper filtering. FAU_SEL.1 enables that filtering.

While very often included in STs, FAU_GEN.1 does pose some challenges because of its varied embedded requirements. Below is the SFR definition from [CC2].

FAU_GEN.1 Audit data generation

Hierarchical to: No other components.
Dependencies: FPT_STM.1 Reliable time stamps

FAU_GEN.1.1   The TSF shall be able to generate an audit record of the following auditable events:
a) Start-up and shutdown of the audit functions;
b) All auditable events for the [selection, choose one of: minimum, basic, detailed, not specified] level of audit; and
c) [assignment: other specifically defined auditable events].

FAU_GEN.1.2   The TSF shall record within each audit record at least the following information:
a) Date and time of the event, type of event, subject identity (if applicable), and the outcome (success or failure) of the event; and
b) For each audit event type, based on the auditable event definitions of the functional components included in the PP/ST, [assignment: other audit relevant information].

For software-only TOEs, the dependency on FPT_STM.1 Reliable time stamps is often met by an Assumption and Objective of the Operational Environment to provide a system clock. See more on this in the discussion about FPT_STM.1 later in this chapter.

Events that may be used to indicate the start-up and shutdown of the audit functions are the initialization and shutdown of the TOE. These may be the commands from an administrator to initiate these actions. If the TOE records these events, then this part of FAU_GEN.1 is satisfied.

Another requirement to carefully consider with FAU_GEN.1 is the fact that if this SFR is claimed, then all of the audit requirements defined by any other SFR in the ST must be met. For example, [CC2] defines the FMT_MOF.1 Management of security functions behavior. FMT_MOF.1 has an audit requirement that states "All modifications in the behaviour of the functions in the TSF." This means that when an administrator makes a configuration change to a security parameter, that change must be logged. If the TOE includes FMT_MOF.1, then the TOE must audit all changes made to the security parameters mentioned in FMT_MOF.1. Many STs claim the "not specified" level of audit (in FAU_GEN.1.1) but evaluators still expect that all of the audit requirements from the other SFRs will be met.

The key requirement in FAU_GEN.1 to consider is the requirement to record the date and time of the event, the subject, and outcome (success or failure) of the event. The TOE must log all of these items in the audit record for each covered event.

Usually, products that log events and satisfy FAU_GEN.1 also provide the capability to review those logs and could also satisfy FAU_SAR.1 Audit review. Some products however do not by themselves provide the functionality to review the logs. For example, products may log events to the Microsoft Windows security event log. To review the Windows security event log, users usually use the Microsoft Windows Event Viewer utility. Unless the Windows operating system is part of the TOE (not generally recommended), the Event Viewer is outside the scope of the TOE. SFRs can only be attributed to the TOE so in this instance this SFR cannot be claimed. FAU_SAR.1 requirements are fairly simple and straight-forward so TOEs that provide even a rudimentary audit log viewer may be able to satisfy this requirement. However, FAU_SAR.1 requires that an event is logged to indicate when a user reviews the audit log which is uncommon.

FAU_STG.1, FAU_STG.2, FAU_STG.3, and FAU_STG.4 all have requirements for protecting the audit log storage. Unless the TOE has its own database or file system within its scope, these SFRs are difficult to claim. TOEs that use external databases or file systems to store audit records should not claim these SFRs. The protection mechanism must be within the scope and control of the TOE. This is not going to be the case for products that rely on external databases and file systems to store the audit records.

Cryptographic Support (FCS)

The Cryptographic Support (FCS) class of SFRs is where the Common Criteria overlaps the National Institute of Science and Technology's (NIST) Federal Information Processing Standard 140-2 (FIPS 140-2) Cryptographic Module Validation Program (CMVP). The FIPS 140-2 validation helps ensure that a cryptographic module (hardware, software, or a combination) has correctly implemented standard cryptographic algorithms and functions. Cryptographic modules may be chips, circuit boards, appliances, or software libraries. These modules may be incorporated into TOEs that implement higher-level security functions that use the cryptographic functions provided by these modules. For example, a VPN router may implement secure socket layer (SSL) communications which uses Advanced Encryption Standard (AES) encryption and Hashed Message Authentication Code (HMAC) provided by a cryptographic module.

While FIPS 140-2 is not required for a CC evaluation claiming SFRs from the FCS class, the information gathered during the FIPS validation can provide the information needed to respond to the FCS requirements.

The best way to satisfy the FCS SFR requirements is to first gain a clear understanding of how the TOE uses cryptography. Encryption and decryption as well as digital signatures and message authentication are used in many Internet communications protocols such as SSL, TLS, and HTTPS. These communication protocols are used for functions such as sending and receiving configuration settings from the administrator's web-based management console (web browser) or securely sending audit log data to an external syslog server. FTP_TRP.1 is an SFR in the FTP Trusted Path/Channels class and specifies that a trusted path shall be used to communicate with remote users. That trusted path may be an HTTPS connection to a web browser used by an administrator. HTTPS uses the cryptographic functions that should be claimed from the FCS class of SFRs.

The FCS class of SFRs covers key management and cryptographic operations. Key management (FCS_CKM) covers the key generation/destruction, distribution and import processes. Keys are either generated by the TOE or input to the TOE from some external source; one method needs to be selected and defined by the appropriate SFR. These keys will be used by some cryptographic operation that must be claimed in an FCS_COP.1 Cryptographic Operation SFR. FCS_COP.1 is defined as:

FCS_COP.1.1   The TSF shall perform [*assignment: list of cryptographic operations*] in accordance with a specified cryptographic algorithm [*assignment: cryptographic algorithm*] and cryptographic key sizes [*assignment: cryptographic key*

40

sizes] that meet the following: [*assignment: list of standards*].

FCS_COP.1 Cryptographic Operation is usually iterated that is, there will oftentimes be FCS_COP.1(1), FCS_COP.1(2), etc. to define the various cryptographic operations supported by the TOE. These operations may include encryption/decryption, digital signatures, hashing, message authentication, and random bit generation. For each iteration, the Assignment clauses are completed with the applicable operations, algorithms, key sizes, and standards. Essentially any operation that can be defined in the FIPS 140-2 validation may be claimed as long as they are used by some higher-level security functions provided by the TOE and included in the ST.

Knowing what cryptographic standards are supported by the TOE is important for completing the definitions of the FCS SFR claims. This information can come from the FIPS 140-2 validation documents.

User Data Protection (FDP)

The User Data Protection (FDP) class contains a strange collection of SFRs but the ones I've found most applicable to commercial products are:

- FDP_ACC.1 Subset access control
- FDP_ACF.1 Security attribute based access control
- FDP_IFC.1 Subset information flow control
- FDP_IFF.1 Simple security attributes
- FDP_ITT.1 Basic internal transfer protection

The FDP_ACC.1 Subset access control and FDP_ACF.1 Security attribute based access control are dependent upon one another so both have to be included in the ST. They are commonly found in commercial product STs because they can easily be applied to the fact that administrators have access privileges to the TOE management functions. I've found the terminology used in these SFRs to be confusing because they are so abstract. Subjects, objects, and security attributes need to be carefully considered when defining these SFRs and how they apply to the TOE.

While FDP_ACC.1 does not have any Management or Audit requirements, FDP_ACF.1 does. It also has a dependency on FMT_MSA.3 Static attribute initialization which requires that a specified user (presumably an administrator) shall be able to change the system default

41

values for the parameters affected by FDP_ACC.1 and FDP_ACF.1. In my experience most commercial products do not allow administrators to set default values. So while many products satisfy the FDP_ACC.1 and FDP_ACF.1 standalone requirements, many do not satisfy the FMT_MSA.3 requirements. See the discussion about FMT_MSA.3 in the Security Management section of this chapter.

FDP_IFC.1 Subset information flow control and FDP_IFF.1 Simple security attributes are similar to the FDP_ACC.1 and FDP_ACF.1 pair in that they are dependent upon one another, FDP_IFF.1 has management and audit requirements as well as the FMT_MSA.3 requirement. These SFRs are most applicable to products that control the flow of data such as firewalls or virtual private networks (VPN). FDP_IFF.1 enforces information flow control policies which can be equated to firewall rules or VPN policies.

FDP_ITT.1 Basic internal transfer protection describes the secure communications used between distributed parts of the TOE. This SFR is useful for TOEs that are composed of a client and server and use protected communications between them. It is dependent upon either FDP_ACF.1 or FDP_IFF.1 which means FMT_MSA.3 must also be included. As mentioned in the Cryptographic Support discussion, there should be associated cryptographic functions defined if FDP_ITT.1 is claimed.

Identification and Authentication (FIA)

FIA_UAU.1 Timing of authentication and FIA_UID.1 Timing of identification are very commonly-used SFRs as they reflect the fact that most commercial products require the administrator to login to the TOE in order to gain access to any of its functions. The login process covers the identification and authentication requirements. Many products not only require logins with credentials (e.g., user name and password), they also associate the user with a set of privileges and roles. The management of these parameters satisfies the management requirements for FIA_UAU.1 and requires an SFR in Security Management (FMT) to manage user data. It is also very common for commercial products to record login events which satisfy the audit requirements of both SFRs.

The other FIA_UAU SFRs provide for defining additional authentication features that a TOE may claim. These are infrequently used however.

Security Management (FMT)

I find the SFRs in the Security Management (FMT) class sometimes confusing because terminology used is intended to be generic. At times it takes extra effort to map the terms and characteristics of the TOE's management (i.e., configuration) functions to the FMT SFR requirements and terms.

All of the SFRs in the FMT class have audit requirements because maintaining the forensic trail of activities conducted by those that configure the TOE is considered critical to security in the eyes of CC. All of the changes made by authorized users shall be audited.

All of the popular FMT SFRs have dependencies on FMT_SMR.1 Security roles and FMT_SMF.1 Specification of Management Functions which make sense as these SFRs define the need to configure and manage different user roles and privileges.

FMT_MSA.1 Management of security attributes is another popular Security Management SFR and is defined as:

FMT_MSA.1.1 The TSF shall enforce the [*assignment: access control SFP(s), information flow control SFP(s)*] to restrict the ability to [selection: change default, query, modify, de-lete, *[assignment: other operations]*] the security attributes [*assignment: list of security attributes*] to [*assignment: the authorised identified roles*].

This SFR illustrates the use of the SFR operations: Assignment and Selection. An Assignment operation occurs where a parameter may be set by the ST author. The Selection operation occurs where the ST author selects one or more items from the given list. Formatting was added to this example to highlight the different operations.

FMT_MSA.1 has dependencies on FDP_ACF.1 (Access Control) or FDP_IFF.1 (Information Flow Control) depending on whether FMT_MSA.1 relates to the attributes associated with an Access Control Security Function Policy (SFP) or an Information Flow Control SFP. It has dependencies on FMT_SMF.1 and FMT_SMR.1 because it requires that a particular user role with the right permissions is allowed to perform the designated operations.

An example of FMT_MSA.1 is shown below:

FMT_MSA.1.1 The TSF shall enforce the *Firewall Information Control Policy* to restrict the ability to query, modify or delete the security attributes *associated with protected resources which are used for access control permission rules* to the Administrator.

This SFR claims that the TOE will only allow Administrators to query, modify, or delete the security attributes (i.e., network traffic rule parameter values) associated with protected resources in accordance with the Firewall Information Control Policy. The Firewall Information Flow Control Policy should be defined in FDP_IFF.1.

As I mentioned earlier, FMT_MSA.3 - Static attribute initialisation is a dependency for many key SFRs including several FDP User Data Protection functions. The problem with FMT_MSA.3 is that many commercial products do not meet all of the requirements of this SFR as illustrated below.

FMT_MSA.3 Static attribute initialisation

FMT_MSA.3.1 The TSF shall enforce the [assignment: access control SFP, information flow control SFP] to provide [selection, choose one of: restrictive, permissive, [assignment: other property]] default values for security attributes that are used to enforce the SFP.

FMT_MSA.3.2 The TSF shall allow the [assignment: the authorised identified roles] to specify alternative initial values to override the default values when an object or information is created.

Many commercial products meet FMT_MSA.3.1 by providing "restrictive" default values for their access controls or information flow controls by denying access by default. For example, firewalls generally require that a rule needs to be defined to allow network traffic to flow otherwise the traffic is blocked. The default (by omission) is restrictive by preventing traffic from flowing. The same method is usually applied to access controls by only allowing explicitly granted permissions for access to resources.

FMT_MSA.3.2 poses a problem for most products because this SFR requires the ability to change default values. In my experience, most products do not allow this nor is it typically advised. I have argued that it is more secure to not allow a user (presumably an administrator) to change the default. In these cases, a Refinement on the SFR may be justified. I recommend a Refinement over an Extended Component because it is easier to document and evaluate. Below is an example of the refinement with **bold** text highlighting the changes.

FMT_MSA.3.2 **Refinement**: The TSF shall **not** allow the *Administrator* role to specify alternative initial values to override the default values when an object or information is created.

Application Note: Allowing Administrators to change default values reduces the predictability and security of the configuration settings. The refinement of this SFR is made to ensure greater control over the initial values.

I think of the FMT_MTD.1 SFR as a more generic form of FMT_MSA.1 in that it deals with any TSF Data, not just those associated with access control policies or information flow control policies and thus is not dependent upon the FDP SFRs. FMT_MTD.1 states:

FMT_MTD.1.1 The TSF shall restrict the ability to [selection: change default, query, modify, delete, clear, [*assignment: other operations*]] the [*assignment: list of TSF data*] to [*assignment: the authorised identified roles*].

The CC standards assume that the TOE will have users with different permissions such as operators, who can only execute operational commands and administrators, who are granted access to configuration functions. FMT_SMF.1 and FMT_SMR.1 are used to define the supported user roles and their set of permissions. As mentioned earlier, most of the FMT SFRs have dependencies on these two SFRs and thus must also be included in the ST.

Protection of the TOE Security Function (FPT)

The Protection of TOE Security Function (TSF) (FPT) class includes requirements that help ensure the integrity and management of the functions of the TOE and the integrity of TOE data. While requirements in the FPT class may appear to duplicate those in the FDP: User data protection class; FDP focuses on user data protection, while FPT focuses on TSF data protection. The FPT class provides requirements that the TOE security policies cannot be tampered with or bypassed. The information provided in these SFRs will be useful when developing the

45

Security Architecture document. See Chapter 14: Security Architecture for more details.

Many of the more commonly used SFRs in this class have to do with maintaining the security of transmitted data.

FPT_ITC.1 Inter-TSF confidentiality during transmission is a simple SFR with no audit or management requirements. It merely states that the TOE will protect TOE data transmitted to an external IT product such as a syslog server or external database. While this SFR has no formal dependencies, in order to protect data transmissions the TOE must use some kind of trusted channel (e.g., SSL) which is supported by some cryptographic functions. This indicates that SFRs from the FTP: Trusted Path/Channels class and FCS: Cryptographic Support class should also be included.

FPT_ITT.1 Basic internal TSF data transfer protection is the intra-TOE analogy to FPT_ITC.1 except that the SFR includes a selection of specifying either protecting from "disclosure and/or modification" of data whereas FPT_ITC.1 merely states "protect" data. Protecting from disclosure implies the use of some form of data encryption. Protection from modification may require the use of digital signatures.

Date and timestamps in audit records are required. That is why FAU_GEN.1 Audit data generation has a dependency on FPT_STM.1 Reliable time stamps. This SFR merely states that the TOE "shall be able to provide reliable time stamps." With many commercial products especially application software products, timestamps are retrieved from the operating system or Network Time Protocol (NTP) servers or something else outside the TOE boundary. The dependency for FAU_GEN.1 can be met with an explanation in the rationale section of the ST and an Assumption and Objective of the Operational Environment that states that a reliable clock will be made available to the TOE.

The FPT_TST.1 TSF testing SFR is commonly used with TOEs that include a FIPS 140-2 validated cryptographic module because FIPS 140-2 requires that the module be able to perform power-on self-tests. FPT_TST.1 states:

FPT_TST.1.1 The TSF shall run a suite of self tests [selection: during initial start-up, periodically during normal operation, at the request of the authorised user, at the conditions[assignment: conditions under which self test should occur]] to demonstrate the correct operation of [selection: [assignment: parts of TSF], the TSF].

46

FPT_TST.1.2   The TSF shall provide authorised users with the capabil-
              ity to verify the integrity of [selection: [*assignment: parts
              of TSF data*], TSF data].
FPT_TST.1.3   The TSF shall provide authorised users with the capabil-
              ity to verify the integrity of [selection: [*assignment: parts
              of TSF*], TSF].

For TOEs that include a FIPS 140-2 validated module, self-tests
may be executed on the cryptographic module portion of the TOE at
start-up or on command to verify the integrity of the cryptographic
module (e.g., parts of TSF) and data passing through it (e.g., parts of TSF
data).

To fully satisfy the FPT_TST.1 requirements, he TOE needs to
record the self-test execution events along with the test results.

Trusted Path/Channels (FTP)

There are two SFRs in the Trusted Path/Channels (FTP) class. A
trusted channel is a secured communications connection between the
TOE and an external IT entity. A trusted path is a secured communications mechanism between the TOE and its users.

Both SFRs have audit requirements and as expected, they both
have management requirements to configure the communications
parameters.

The Trusted Path/Channel SFRs need to be defined consistently
with the FPT Protection of the TSF and FCS Cryptographic Support
SFRs. If there is an SFR from FPT claiming to protect the communications between the TOE and an outside IT product, then the Trusted
Channel FTP_ITC.1 SFR should be included. If the TOE supports remote
user access to TOE functions, then FTP_TRP.1 Trusted Path should be
claimed.

If either FTP_ITC.1 or FTP_TRP.1 is claimed, then the supporting
cryptographic functions used by the communications mechanisms need
to be covered in the FCS_COP.1 Cryptographic operation SFRs.

For example, many commercial products use web browser-based
administrator consoles to manage the product. These web browsers
support Hypertext Transport Protocol Secure (HTTPS). HTTPS in turn
uses Secure Socket Layer (SSL) or Transport Layer Security (TLS) to
secure the communications path. SSL and TLS use a variety of cryptographic functions such as encryption, decryption, digital signatures,
hashing, and message authentication. These algorithms in turn use key

47

generation, distribution, and destruction mechanisms to manage the cryptographic keys.

Minimize TOE Scope

Commercial products contain many features – some security-related. It is tempting (from a marketing point of view) to attempt to incorporate as many competitive or differentiating features into the evaluation as possible. There is a simple axiom that applies to all CC evaluations – the larger the scope, the longer it takes and the greater the risk of failure. Introducing unnecessary features into the scope of the evaluation increase the risk that the evaluation will not be successfully completed. This is why I advocate that developers should strive to minimize the scope of the evaluation by being judicious in their selection of security functions to include in the evaluation. This essentially equates to minimizing the number of SFRs claimed in the ST.

Each security function that is claimed within the TOE will need to be documented and tested. The bulk of that documentation will lay in the Development Assurance (ADV) documentation. Details of those documents are discussed in Part IV: Development. Even at Evaluation Assurance Level 2 (EAL2), all security functions will need to be tested. A test plan with detailed test procedures will need to be developed and test results will need to be recorded to satisfy the Test Assurance (ATE) requirements. Part VI: Testing covers the details of the ATE requirements. Increasing the number of SFRs increases the document development effort as well as the evaluation and testing effort. To quickly, efficiently, and successfully complete the CC evaluation carefully consider what security functions (i.e., SFRs) to include in the TOE Boundary.

Analogous to the argument to reduce security function claims is the argument to reduce security assurance scope. Each CC evaluation must be performed to some set of security assurance requirements. CC has conveniently provided collections or packages of these assurance claims into Evaluation Assurance Levels (EALs). Developers usually select the targeted EAL based on customer demand or competitive pressures. Most commercial products have selected either EAL2 or EAL4.

In my experience, any successful commercial vendor can meet EAL2 requirements without making any significant changes to their development, delivery, or support processes. EAL2 documentation efforts are also fairly straight-forward to complete without undue

48

burden on the development staff. The assurance requirements for EAL2 are summarized in Table 1 - EAL2 Assurance Requirements

EAL4 requires considerably more time and effort – definitely more than twice that of EAL2. The requirements for EAL4 are shown in Table 2 - EAL4 Assurance Requirements. Compared to EAL2, EAL4 requires several additional process documents such as Design Security, Tools and Techniques, and Lifecycle Process. Also, there is significantly more detail required in the ADV documents for EAL4. The ADV demands are particularly problematic because of the significant burden it places on the people who know the most about the internal workings of the TOE. Usually those people are in the greatest demand and have the least amount of available time.

As I mentioned earlier, commercial product developers frequently augment their EAL2 or EAL4 evaluations with Flaw Remediation. Augmentation means that additional assurance (i.e., documentation) requirements are added to the standard EAL requirements. Flaw Remediation covers the developers defect tracking and management processes. Since most commercial product developers have documented defect tracking and management processes, it is easy (and cheap) to add Flaw Remediation to their CC evaluation. See more on this topic in Chapter 11: Flaw Remediation (+).

Minimize System Configurations

Developers have the choice of selecting the platforms that will be considered supported platforms for the purposes of the CC evaluation. Platforms are the hardware and software components that are outside the TOE but are required in order for the TOE to operate. For example, application software requires computer hardware including processors, memory, and disk drives. In addition, applications may execute on top of an operating system or middleware. All of these items are considered platform components for the CC evaluation.

Commercial products oftentimes are supported on a variety of platforms. For example, RSA, The Security Division of EMC, Access Manager v6.1 advertises support for Microsoft Windows Server, Oracle/Sun Solaris, Red Hat Linux, SUSE Linux, and IBM AIX. The product documentation also claims support for a variety of middleware that Access Manager relies upon to perform its functions. This variety of platforms is supported to meet customer demand and remain competitive.

The supported platforms listed in the Security Target for RSA Access Manager v6.1 only includes Windows Server 2003 and Solaris 10 operating systems. There are similar limitations on the middleware supported. The most common reason to limit the number of platforms for the CC evaluation is that fewer platforms means less testing effort which reduces the overall time-to-market (TTM) for a CC evaluated product. Improving the TTM can have a positive impact on company revenues. Conversely, adding platforms increases time, effort, and schedule risk that can have a negative impact on revenues.

About Protection Profiles

Developers are given the choice of evaluating their products against security claims they make or evaluating against the requirements in a published Protection Profile (PP). Protection Profiles apply to a product or technology type and are designed to reflect the requirements of a set of users of the technology. PPs contain the security functional requirements (SFRs) and a specific Evaluation Assurance Level (EAL) expected to be evaluated by products fitting the product type covered by the PP.

Developers generally choose to evaluate their product against their own security claims rather than PPs because it gives them more flexibility. In many cases, PP conformance may be too restrictive for developers of existing products.

Most developers I've encountered who have chosen to evaluate against the requirements in a PP have done so because their customers have specifically demanded it. Of those, several have had to implement new features or have had to modify existing functionality to meet the PP requirements.

My advice is that if a developer chooses to claim conformance to a PP, they should conduct a "gap analysis" by very carefully comparing the PP requirements with their product's capabilities. This "gap analysis" should yield a clear understanding of what existing product features will meet the functional requirements and where the product falls short. Any functional gaps will need to be addressed with product modifications or a detailed rationale explaining the deficiency.

I have had clients promise their customers that their product will conform to a PP before conducting a "gap analysis" and eventually terminating the evaluation because of lack of allocated resources to make the product changes necessary.

Chapter 5: Security Target

The Security Target (ST) document is the foundational document for all Common Criteria evaluations. Its purpose is to frame the scope of the evaluation. It defines the Target of Evaluation (TOE) and the Operational Environment in which the TOE is to be deployed in a secure fashion. The content and format of the ST is the same for EAL2 and EAL4. The Security Target assurance (ASE) requirements are summarized in the following table.

ASSURANCE CLASS	COMPONENTS
ASE: Security Target	ASE_INT.1 ST introduction
	ASE_CCL.1 Conformance claims
	ASE_SPD.1 Security problem definition
	ASE_OBJ.2 Security objectives
	ASE_ECD.1 Extended components definition
	ASE_REQ.2 Derived security requirements
	ASE_TSS.1 TOE summary specification

Table 3 - ASE Requirements

The ST document must satisfy the ASE assurance requirements defined in [CC3]. The following ST outline may be used to address all of the ASE documentation requirements.
- Document Overview
- Introduction
  - ST Reference
  - TOE Reference
  - TOE Overview
  - TOE Description
- Conformance Claims
  - CC Version
  - PP Conformance Claims
- Security Problem Definition
  - Assets
  - Threats
  - Organizational Security Policies
  - Assumptions

- Security Objectives
  - o Security Objectives of the TOE
  - o Security Objectives of the Operational Environ-ment
  - o Security Objectives Rationale
- Extended Components Definition
- Security Requirements
  - o Security Functional Requirements
  - o Security Assurance Requirements
  - o Security Requirements Rationale
- TOE Summary Specifications
  - o Security Functions
  - o TOE Security Specifications

This chapter will describe each section of the ST and explain the content that satisfies each of the ASE assurance requirements.

Document Overview

While not a specific requirement called out in the CC standards, it is customary (and convenient) to include an introductory section that provides an overview of the Security Target formatting conventions and layout. The Document Overview section usually includes:
- Abstract
- Table of contents
- Table of tables
- Table of figures
- Document organization
- Document formatting conventions
- Glossary of terms

Abstract

The Abstract is a summary of the ST presenting a very high-level explanation of the purpose of the document. Below is an example of an ST abstract.

This document provides the basis for an evaluation of a specific Target of Evaluation (TOE), Securitee Inc. CyberSleuth v2.0. This Security Target (ST) defines a set of assumptions about the operational environment, a list of threats that the product intends to counter, a set of security objectives, a set of security requirements and the IT security functions provided by the TOE which meet the set of security objectives.

Tables

The Table of Contents lists the ST sections and subsections and their associated page numbers. The Table of Tables and Table of Figures provide the page numbers for the tables and figures used in the ST. These tables make it easier to locate specific items in the ST which come in handy during document editing and review sessions.

Document Organization

The Document Organization summarizes the various ST sections.

SECTION	TITLE	DESCRIPTION
1	ST Introduction	Includes an overview and description of the TOE, the hardware and software that make up the TOE, as well as the physical and logical boundaries of the TOE
2	Conformance Claims	Lists evaluation conformance to Common Criteria versions and applicable Protection Profiles and Packages.
3	Security Problem Definition	Specifies the assets, threats, assumptions and organizational security policies that affect the TOE.
4	Security Objectives	Defines the security objectives for the TOE and operational environment and rationale illustrating that the security objectives mitigate the threats.
5	Extended Components Definition	Details any extended components used in this evaluation.
6	Security Requirements	Describes the functional and assurance requirements for this TOE.
7	TOE Summary Specification	Identifies the IT security functions provided by the TOE and how the assurance requirements are satisfied.

Table 4 - ST Document Organization

Document Formatting Conventions

Document Formatting Conventions are provided to help readers identify the different constructs used in the Security Target. An example of document formatting conventions is presented below. While these formatting conventions are not required, they may be helpful to the reader (e.g., evaluator) to more quickly identify these special items.

The notation, formatting, and conventions of Security Functional Requirements (SFR) used in Section 6: Security Requirements are used to highlight operations defined in Part 2 of the Common Criteria. These operations are refinement, selection, assignment , assignment within a selection, and iteration. Also, extended SFRs have special identifiers. The notation for each operation is shown below.

- Assignment: Indicated with *italicized* text;
- Refinement made by PP author: Indicated with **bold** text and ~~strikethroughs~~, if necessary;
- Selection: Indicated with <u>underlined</u> text;
- Assignment within a Selection: Indicated with *<u>italicized and underlined</u>* text;
- Iteration: Indicated by appending the iteration number in parenthesis, e.g., (1), (2), (3) to the SFR.
- Extended components: Indicated with _EXT suffix as with FAU_STG_EXT.1.

Section 3: Security Problem Definition of this Security Target defines the Assumptions, Threats, and Organizational Security Policies applicable to the TOE. These items use the following naming conventions:

- Assumptions are denoted A.assumption,
- Threats are denoted T.threat,
- Policies are denoted P.policy.

Section 5: Security Objectives defines the Objectives for the TOE and the Operational Environment. These objectives are identified using the following format:

- TOE Objectives are denoted O.objective,
- Objectives for the Operational Environment are denoted OE.objective.

Glossary of Terms

The Glossary of Terms provides a useful reference for acronyms and abbreviations used throughout the ST. Use of acronyms and abbreviations reduces the length of the document. Below is an example of a glossary of commonly used CC terms. ST glossaries generally also include product-specific or technology-specific terms used in the ST.

TERM	DEFINITION
CC	Common Criteria version 3.1
EAL	Evaluation Assurance Level
HTTPS	Hyper Text Transport Protocol Secure
OSP	Organizational Security Policy
SFP	Security Function Policy
SFR	Security Functional Requirement
ST	Security Target
TLS	Transport Layer Security
TOE	Target of Evaluation
TSF	TOE Security Function

Table 5 - Sample Glossary

Section 1: ST Introduction

Section 1 of the ST is the ST Introduction. This section addresses the following Security Target Evaluation Assurance (ASE) requirements as defined in [CC3]. The table below illustrates the ASE requirements for the ST Introduction.

ASE_INT.1 ST introduction

DEVELOPER ACTION ELEMENT	DESCRIPTION
ASE_INT.1.1D	The developer shall provide an ST introduction.
CONTENT AND PRESENTATION ELEMENTS	**DESCRIPTION**
ASE_INT.1.1C	The ST introduction shall contain an ST reference, a TOE reference, a TOE overview and a TOE description. The developer shall provide an ST introduction.
ASE_INT.1.2C	The ST reference shall uniquely identify the ST.
ASE_INT.1.3C	The TOE reference shall identify the TOE.
ASE_INT.1.4C	The TOE overview shall summarise the usage and major security features of the TOE.
ASE_INT.1.5C	The TOE overview shall identify the TOE type.

ASE_INT.1.6C	The TOE overview shall identify any non-TOE hardware/software/firmware required by the TOE.
ASE_INT.1.7C	The TOE description shall describe the physical scope of the TOE.
ASE_INT.1.8C	The TOE description shall describe the logical scope of the TOE.

Table 6 - ASE_INT.1 Requirements

The overall developer action element requirement is met by meeting all of the content and presentation element requirements.

In my opinion, much of the verbiage contained within a Security Target is redundant. The ST Introduction provides a very high-level prosaic description of the TOE security features. The TOE Description, while it includes a description of the physical TOE boundary, is an embellishment upon the TOE Introduction providing the next level of detail to the security functions provided by the TOE. The bulk of the ST resides in Section 6: Security Requirements which are descriptions of the security functions in CC language (e.g., from [CC2]). Finally, the TOE Summary Specifications (TSS) in Section 7 of the ST tries to combine the content of Section 6 with the TOE Description. The TSS is another prosaic description of the TOE security functions mapping product functions to specific SFRs.

If the ST author keeps this redundancy in mind, it can make writing the ST easier as the author can remain focused on the claimed security features and avoid drifting into discussions about extraneous product features that are not relevant to the evaluation.

ST Reference

The ST Reference is a unique identifier associated with the specific ST document. This will address the ST Reference part of ASE_INT.1.1C and all of ASE_INT.1.2C. An example is shown below.

ST Title	Security Target: Securitee Inc. CyberSleuth v2.0
ST Revision	1.2
ST Publication Date	June 7, 2014

TOE Reference

The TOE Reference is the unique identifier for the TOE. This will address the TOE Reference part of ASE_INT.1.1C and all of ASE_INT.1.3C. This will include the company name, product name, and product version identifiers. The philosophy behind the Common Criteria is that it is an evaluation of a "snapshot in time" of a product. The binary code and hardware components that make up the product are frozen for the purposes of this evaluation. The CC certificate is issued for that precise frozen set of hardware and software. The TOE Reference gives the unique name to this set of hardware and software that compose the TOE.

Product version identification varies from company-to-company but the idea behind the TOE Reference is to enable the evaluator, certifier, and customer to precisely identify the evaluated version of the product. This usually means that at a minimum the product version number must be specified in the TOE Reference. The version number may include a patch level depending on how the developer designates patches. Many evaluators expect to see build numbers or release dates in the TOE Reference. An example of a TOE Reference is shown below.

TOE Reference: Securitee Inc. CyberSleuth v2.0 Build 20140604

TOE Overview

The TOE Overview provides a brief overview of the main TOE security functions and defines the TOE Type. The TOE Type is a very brief, general description of the TOE's primary function. The ST author may select a TOE Type from the general types listed on the Common Criteria Portal [Portal] website's listing of certified products and include this in the TOE Overview.

The TOE Overview will satisfy the TOE Overview part of ASE_INT.1.1C and all of ASE_INT.1.4C and ASE_INT.1.5C. The description of the non-TOE hardware and software required to satisfy ASE_INT.1.6C is oftentimes better covered in the TOE Description section of the ST which describes the physical TOE boundary. A brief example of a TOE Overview is given here.

The Securitee Inc. CyberSleuth v2.0 (referred to as the TOE) is an access control system designed for enterprise-wide deployments. The TOE is deployed in software-only form or in an appliance provided by

Securitee Inc.. The TOE's primary function is to manage external user access to controlled computing resources such as intranet web servers and corporate email servers. The TOE allows remote users access to controlled resources based on administrator-defined access policies. Administrators gain access to TOE management functions through a web-based console that uses HTTPS to the TOE server.

The TOE Overview need only be a few paragraphs long. The TOE Description should carry more of the details about the TOE. Some ST authors like to use the TOE Overview as a marketing vehicle to promote more of the product's (non-security) functions. This practice is generally discouraged by evaluators and certifiers. Remember that the ST provides the framework for the CC evaluation and focusses attention on the specific security claims made in the rest of the document. CC evaluations and the ST are all about "security functionality." In the context of CC and the creation of the ST, "security functionality" means the security functional claims made in the ST and detailed in Section 6: Security Requirements of the ST.

TOE Description

The TOE Description expands on the content provided in the TOE Overview. The TOE Description may be several pages long describing the security functionality of the TOE. In addition, the TOE Description addresses the ASE_INT.1.7C and ASE_INT.1.8C requirements by describing the physical and logical scope of the TOE. As mentioned earlier, the description of the non-TOE hardware and software required to satisfy ASE_INT.1.6C is oftentimes better covered in this section of the ST in the context of the physical boundary of the TOE.

I have found that high-level block diagrams of the TOE are extremely useful in the TOE Description. In some cases, multiple diagrams are necessary to illustrate the different TOE configurations covered by the evaluation. The example given for the TOE Overview above explains that the "The TOE is deployed in software-only form or in an appliance provided by Securitee Inc." There should be a diagram illustrating the software-only version of Securitee Inc. CyberSleuth v2.0 and another diagram showing the appliance version of the product. These diagrams should make it clear what hardware and software is part of the TOE and what hardware and software is part of the Operational Environment. The Operational Environment is basically anything the TOE relies upon in order to function but is not part of the TOE itself. Typical examples of parts of the Operational Environment are operating systems and general-purpose computers on which the TOE application software executes.

The diagram below is a sample of the appliance configuration of the TOE.

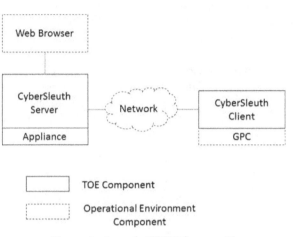

Figure 4 - Sample TOE Diagram #1

Below is a sample diagram of the TOE in the configuration using a general purpose computer (GPC).

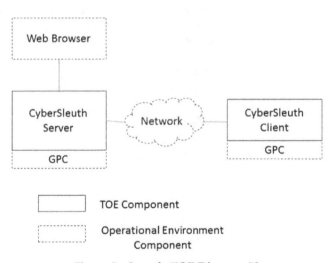

Figure 5 - Sample TOE Diagram #2

59

These diagram plus the written details of the TOE and non-TOE components satisfies the ASE_INT.1.7C requirement. A simple (and clear) way to explain the hardware and software requirements of the TOE and the Operational Environment (i.e., non-TOE) is to provide a table for each component with the component name (consistent with the names used in the diagrams) and the details of the hardware and software used. Below are examples of TOE component hardware and software descriptions.

The TOE is composed of two components: SuperStealth Server and SuperStealth Client. The SuperStealth Server may be deployed in an appliance configuration as well as a software configuration. The hardware and software requirements for the SuperStealth Server are described in the table below.

REQUIREMENT	DETAILS
TOE Software	Securitee Inc. CyberSleuth v2.0
Appliance Hardware	Securitee Inc. CyberSleuth v2.0 Appliance
General Purpose Computer (GPC) Hardware	x86-64 bit Dual CPU 16 MB RAM 100 GB of disk space
General Purpose Computer (GPC) Software	Microsoft Windows Server 2008 R2 Red Hat Linux 6.0 Oracle Java JRE 6.0

The SuperStealth Client is a software application that executes on general purpose computers. The hardware and software requirements for the SuperStealth Client are described in the table below.

REQUIREMENT	DETAILS
TOE Software	Securitee Inc. CyberSleuth v2.0
General Purpose Computer (GPC) Hardware	x86-64 bit Dual CPU 8 MB RAM 20 GB of disk space
General Purpose Computer (GPC) Software	Microsoft Windows 7 Oracle Java JRE 6.0

A similar approach can be taken to explain the hardware and software requirements for the Operational Environment (non-TOE) requirements. Here is an example.

60

Administrator access to the TOE management functions is through a web-based console. The requirements for the web browser are given in the table below.

REQUIREMENT	DETAILS
Web Browser	Mozilla Firefox 12 and higher
	Microsoft Internet Explorer 6.0 and higher
General Purpose Computer (GPC) Hardware	Any system that supports the above web browser.
General Purpose Computer (GPC) Software	Any operating system that supports the above web browser.

What is considered part of the TOE and what is considered part of the Operational Environment is a key question that must be considered when defining the TOE Boundary and completing this section of the ST. Generally speaking, if a component (software or hardware) is required to provide the claimed security functionality in the product, then it needs to be part of the TOE. This becomes a sticky question when third-party components are used. For example, clearly if a database is expected to already be in place (and the TOE does not ship with a database), that database is part of the Operational Environment. What is less clear is if that database is integrated with the TOE but the integrator does not control the database software. At EAL4, where some source code review may be required (ADV_IMP.1) this may not be possible without special arrangements with the third-party database developer. It may be easiest to remove any security claims that rely on that third-party database functionality.

The logical scope of the TOE requirement (ASE_INT.1.8C) is most effectively addressed in a table of TOE security functional classes (TSF) as defined in [CC2] and a brief description of the security functions provided by the TOE related to those TSFs. Below is an example table.

TSF	DESCRIPTION
Security Audit	The TOE logs user login/logout activity, administrator management actions and user transactions. It also records security events such as failed login attempts, etc.. Audit records can be reviewed by administrators.

TSF	DESCRIPTION
Cryptographic Support	The TOE includes a cryptographic module that provides the primitive cryptographic functions used to support the secure communications features of the TOE.
Identification and Authentication	The TOE enforces user identification and authentication prior to granting access to the TOE functions. Users must successfully authenticate using a unique identifier and password prior to performing any actions on the TOE.
User Data Protection	The TOE enforces discretionary access rules using an access control list with user permissions.
Security Management	The TOE restricts the ability to enable, modify and disable security policy rules and user roles to an authorized administrator. The TOE also provides the functions necessary for effective management of the TOE security functions. Administrators configure the TOE through the Management Console via Web-based connection.
Protection of the TSF	The TOE components protect communications using HTTPS/TLS.
Trusted Path/Channels	The TOE provides HTTPS/TLS capabilities to authorized administrators.

Finally, commercial products generally include a set of product guides such as installation manuals, administrator guides, and user guides. The ST Introduction should include the list of standard product guides included with the product to ensure users install and operate the TOE correctly.

Section 2: Conformance Claims

Section 2 of the ST covers the Conformance Claims for the evaluation. This section addresses the following Security Target Evaluation Assurance (ASE) requirements as defined in [CC3]. The following table describes the Conformance Claims requirements.

ASE_CCL.1 Conformance claims

DEVELOPER ACTION ELEMENT	DESCRIPTION
ASE_CCL.1.1D	The developer shall provide a conformance claim.
ASE_CCL.1.2D	The developer shall provide a conformance claim rationale

CONTENT AND PRESENTATION ELEMENTS	DESCRIPTION
ASE_CCL.1.1C	The conformance claim shall contain a CC conformance claim that identifies the version of the CC to which the ST and the TOE claim conformance.
ASE_CCL.1.2C	The CC conformance claim shall describe the conformance of the ST to CC Part 2 as either CC Part 2 conformant or CC Part 2 extended.
ASE_CCL.1.3C	The CC conformance claim shall describe the conformance of the ST to CC Part 3 as either CC Part 3 conformant or CC Part 3 extended.
ASE_CCL.1.4C	The CC conformance claim shall be consistent with the extended components definition.
ASE_CCL.1.5C	The conformance claim shall identify all PPs and security requirement packages to which the ST claims conformance.
ASE_CCL.1.6C	The conformance claim shall describe any conformance of the ST to a package as either package-conformant or package-augmented.
ASE_CCL.1.7C	The conformance claim rationale shall demonstrate that the TOE type is consistent with the TOE type in the PPs for which conformance is being claimed.
ASE_CCL.1.8C	The conformance claim rationale shall demonstrate that the statement of the security problem definition is consistent with the statement of the security problem definition in the PPs for which conformance is being claimed.

ASE_CCL.1.9C	The conformance claim rationale shall demonstrate that the statement of security objectives is consistent with the statement of security objectives in the PPs for which conformance is being claimed.
ASE_CCL.1.10C	The conformance claim rationale shall demonstrate that the statement of security requirements is consistent with the statement of security requirements in the PPs for which conformance is being claimed.

Table 7 - ASE_CCL.1 Requirements

The developer action element requirements (i.e., ASE_CCL.1.1D and ASE_CCL.1.2D) are met by meeting all of the content and presentation element requirements.

The Conformance Claim requirements can be met by including the following subsections in Section 2 of the ST.

- CC Conformance Claim
- PP Claim
- Package Claim
- Conformance Rationale

CC Conformance Claim

The CC Conformance Claim subsection addresses the ASE_CCL.1.1C - ASE_CCL 1.4C requirements. A simple example of a statement that satisfies these requirements is shown below.

The TOE is Common Criteria for Information Technology Security Evaluation, Version 3.1 Revision 4 (September 2012) Part 2 extended and Part 3 conformant.

The term "extended" in this example means that the ST includes SFRs that are extended from the CC Part 2 [CC2] standard. These extended security functions shall be defined in the ST Section 5: Extended Components Definition.

The term "conformant" in this example means that all of the security assurance requirements (SAR) claimed in this ST come directly from CC Part 3 [CC3] and that there are no customized or non-standard security assurance claims.

The example below shows the conformance claim for an evaluation augmenting the standard EAL package with ALC_FLR.2 Flaw reporting procedures. This means that the developer will produce documentation describing the defect tracking and management processes applicable to the TOE. See Chapter 11: Flaw Remediation (+) for more details on the documentation requirements for Flaw Remediation.

The TOE is Common Criteria for Information Technology Security Evaluation Version 3.1 Revision 4 (September 2012) Part 2 extended and Part 3 conformant and augmented with ALC_FLR.2.

PP Claim

If the TOE does not claim conformance to any protection profiles (PP), then the following statement can be included in the ST to satisfy the ASE_CCL.1.5C requirement.

The TOE does not claim conformance to any protection profiles.

However, if the TOE does claim conformance to protection profiles, then statements similar to the one given below may be used.

The TOE claims demonstrable conformance to the Protection Profile for Authorization Servers, version 1.1, September 14, 2008.

Note that if conformance to a PP is claimed, then the Conformance Rationale subsection must be completed as well.

Package Claim

To address the ASE_CCL.1.6C requirement, generally a statement regarding the Evaluation Assurance Level (EAL) claimed for this evaluation is sufficient. An example is shown below.

The TOE claims conformance to the EAL2 assurance package defined in Part 3 of the Common Criteria Version 3.1 Revision 4 (September 2012). The TOE does not claim conformance to any other packages.

The Common Criteria does allow for the definition of other packages beyond EALs. There are several packages widely used in the smart card industry. If any such packages are claimed, they must be noted along with their version and publication dates.

(PP) Conformance Rationale

ASE_CCL.1.7C – ASE_CCL.1.10C are associated with ASE_CCL.1.5C's claims of conformance to PPs. If there are no claims of conformance to PPs, then the following statement is sufficient.

The TOE does not claim conformance to a Protection Profile thus no conformance rationale is provided.

If conformance to a PP is claimed, then rationale must be provided. Conformance to PPs must be specified as either "strict" or "demonstrable."

As defined in CC Part 1 [CC1], STs that claim "strict" conformance to a PP shall claim that the TOE does at least what is required by the PP but may claim more. Simple statements explaining that the TOE is the same TOE type, covers the same security problem definition, security objectives, and security requirements will suffice.

The TOE type is an access control system, and the TOE type in the PP is stated to be an access control system. The TOE type is therefore consistent with the PP.
The security problem definition in the ST is copied exactly from the PP.
The security objectives in the ST are copied from the PP.
The security requirements in the ST are copied from the PP.

STs claiming "demonstrable" conformance with a PP provide a solution to the generic security problem described in the PP in any way that is equivalent or more restrictive to that described in the PP. If an ST claims "demonstrable" conformance, extensive rationale needs to be provided to explain how the TOE solves the security problem posed in the PP. The "demonstrable" conformance option is not often used.

Section 3: Security Problem Definition

Section 3 of the ST defines the security problem to be addressed by the TOE and the Operational Environment. This section addresses the following Security Target Evaluation Assurance (ASE) requirements as defined in [CC3]. The table below describes the ST Security Problem Definition (SPD) requirements.

The CC standards [CC1] admit that the process of deriving the security problem definition falls outside the scope of the CC but it seems to imply that the ST author first defines the assets, threats, and policies related to the TOE. On the surface, the Security Problem Definition with its use of terms like Threats and Organizational Security Policies could lead developers to think that this is a kind of threat modelling exercise. While threat modelling exercises are useful in identifying vulnerabilities in products, the results of such an exercise may be disappointingly less useful for developing the SPD.

If the ST claims strict conformance to a Protection Profile (PP), then the SPD from the PP must be copied exactly into the ST.

ASE_SPD.1 Security problem definition

DEVELOPER ACTION ELEMENT	DESCRIPTION
ASE_SPD.1.1D	The developer shall provide a security problem definition.
CONTENT AND PRESENTATION ELEMENTS	DESCRIPTION
ASE_SPD.1.1C	The security problem definition shall describe the threats.
ASE_SPD.1.2C	All threats shall be described in terms of a threat agent, an asset, and an adverse action.
ASE_SPD.1.3C	The security problem definition shall describe the Organizational Security Policies (OSP).
ASE_SPD.1.4C	The security problem definition shall describe the assumptions about the operational environment of the TOE.

Table 8 - ASE_SPD.1 Requirements

From my experience, I found it to be more practical to extract the SFRs from the commercial product (either current or planned future release version) first. That is, start by deriving the SFRs from the security features of the product and then develop appropriate TOE Objectives. From there, define the Threats and OSPs that are addressed by the TOE Objectives. Operational Environment Objectives and Assumptions can be defined by the system requirements of the TOE. While this process

67

may not be the way to develop a secure system, it is an easier way to write a Security Target.

The developer action element requirement is met by meeting all of the content and presentation element requirements.

The purpose of this section of the ST is to clearly define the security problem to be addressed by the TOE and the Operational Environment. The Security Problem Definition is described in terms of:

- Threats consisting of an adverse action performed by a threat agent on an asset;
- Organizational Security Policies (OSPs) or security rules, procedures, or guidelines imposed by the organization in the Operational Environment; and
- Assumptions about the Operational Environment in order for the TOE to provide its claimed security functionality.

Assets

The CC requirements do not require a separate discussion about Assets being protected by the TOE, but having this subsection makes the ST more self-consistent. Examples of Assets are confidential user data, system performance, or internal TOE configuration settings. These Assets must be used in the Threat definitions.

Threats

A Threat is an adverse action performed by a threat agent on an asset. Adverse actions influence characteristics of an asset from which that asset derives its value. Threat agents may be best described as types of entities. These statements satisfy ASE_SPD.1.1C and ASE_SPD.1.2C. Examples of threat agents are hackers, users, computer processes, and accidents. Threat agents may be further described by characteristics such as expertise, resources, opportunity, and motivation. An example of a Threat is:

T.HACKER   A paid hacker with substantial expertise and standard equipment could remotely copy confidential files from a company network.

There is no strict requirement to give each Threat an identifier (e.g., T.HACKER in the example) but it seems that this is the norm for most STs that have been produced to date. This identification notation is consistent with the ST Document Formatting Conventions.

Organizational Security Policies

Organizational Security Policies (OSPs) are security rules, procedures, or guidelines imposed by the organization in the Operational Environment. These rules may be in place to satisfy legislative or regulatory requirements. These definitions satisfy ASE_SPD.1.3C. OSPs can apply to the TOE and/or the Operational Environment. Below is an example of an OSP.

P.FIPS   All cryptographic functions used in the organization shall be supported by the use of FIPS 140-2 validated modules.

There is no strict requirement to use the OSP identifier (e.g., P.FIPS in the example) but many STs use this convention. This identification notation is consistent with the ST Document Formatting Conventions.

Assumptions

Assumptions are made only on the Operational Environment in order for the TOE to successfully provide its claimed security functionality. If the TOE is placed in an Operational Environment that does not meet these assumptions, the TOE may not be able to provide the expected security functionality. Assumptions can be on physical characteristics, personnel and networks in the Operational Environment. The Assumption statements satisfy the ASE_SPD.1.4C requirement. For example, the Operational Environment-applicable part of the OSP example used earlier can be stated as an Assumption.

A.FIPS   All cryptographic functions used in the Operational Environment shall be supported by the use of FIPS 140-2 validated modules.

The Assumption identifier notation (e.g., A.FIPS in the example) is consistent with the ST Document Formatting Conventions.

Since TOEs are IT systems that have little control over the behavior of the personnel operating the systems, it is common to see assumptions about personnel in STs.

A.TRUST   Administrators using the TOE are trusted to install and operate the TOE in accordance with documented practices.

Also, for software TOEs that have little control over their physical environment, an assumption about the physical environment is warranted.

A.PHYSICAL   The TOE shall be deployed in a physically secured environment.

Section 4: Security Objectives

Section 3 of the ST describes the Security Problem Definition. The Security Problem Definition is solved by Objectives of the TOE and Objectives of the Operational Environment that are detailed in Section 4: Security Objectives of the ST. CC Part 1 [CC1] uses a diagram similar to the following to illustrate the relationships between Threats, Organizational Security Policies (OSP), Assumptions, and the Objectives of the TOE and Objectives of the Operational Environment. Security Objectives of the TOE drive the Security Functional Requirements (SFRs) that are described in Section 6: Security Requirements of the ST.

If the ST claims strict conformance to a Protection Profile (PP), then the Objectives section from the PP must be copied exactly into the ST.

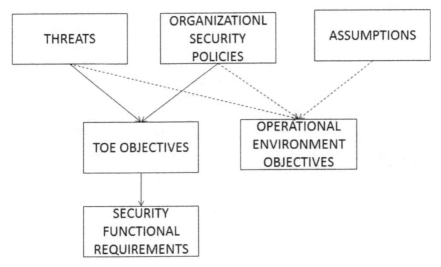

Figure 6 - Objectives Mapping

Section 4 of the ST addresses the Security Target Evaluation Assurance (ASE) requirements as defined in [CC3] for the security objectives to be addressed by the TOE and the Operational Environment. The table below describes the requirements.

ASE_OBJ.2 Security objectives

DEVELOPER ACTION ELEMENT	DESCRIPTION
ASE_OBJ.2.1D	The developer shall provide a statement of security objectives.
CONTENT AND PRESENTATION ELEMENTS	DESCRIPTION
ASE_OBJ.2.1C	The statement of security objectives shall describe the security objectives for the TOE and the security objectives for the operational environment.
ASE_OBJ.2.2C	The security objectives rationale shall trace each security objective for the TOE back to threats countered by that security objective and OSPs enforced by that security objective.

71

ASE_OBJ.2.3C	The security objectives rationale shall trace each security objective for the operational environment back to threats countered by that security objective, OSPs enforced by that security objective, and assumptions upheld by that security objective.
ASE_OBJ.2.4C	The security objectives rationale shall demonstrate that the security objectives counter all threats.
ASE_OBJ.2.5C	The security objectives rationale shall demonstrate that the security objectives enforce all OSPs.
ASE_OBJ.2.6C	The security objectives rationale shall demonstrate that the security objectives for the operational environment uphold all assumptions.

Table 9 - ASE_OBJ.2 Requirements

The developer action element requirements for ASE_OBJ.2 are met by meeting all of the respective content and presentation element requirements.

Security Objectives of the TOE

The Security Objectives of the TOE addresses the TOE Objectives portion of the ASE_OBJ.2.1C requirement. The Security Objectives of the TOE must address all of the Threats defined in the Security Problem Definition. The mitigation of Threats may be shared between the TOE and the Operational Environment but not the Operational Environment alone. An example of how a Threat can be addressed by both the TOE and the Operational Environment is:

T.SNOOP   An attacker sniffs network packets to gain access to confidential user data.

To address this Threat, the TOE implements Secure Socket Layer (SSL) communications when sending sensitive data to trusted external IT servers. Meanwhile, the external servers must also implement those same communications protocols in order to interoperate securely with the TOE. The applicable Objectives for the example would be:

72

O.SSL   The TOE implements the SSL protocol when transmitting customer data to external IT entities.

OE.SSL   The Operational Environment implements the SSL protocol when communicating with the TOE.

Note that the Objectives have identifiers that meet the naming conventions defined in the Security Target.

Security Objectives of the Operational Environment

The Security Objectives of the Operational Environment addresses the Objectives of the Operational Environment portion of the ASE_OBJ.2.1C requirement. All of the Assumptions and the applicable portions of any Organizational Security Policies (OSP) and Threats are addressed by the Objectives of the Operational Environment.

The Operational Environment is outside the scope of the TOE and therefore cannot completely address any Threats or Organizational Security Policies. The earlier example illustrating how the T.SNOOP threat is mitigated by a combination of O.SSL and OE.SSL demonstrates how the combination of Security Objective of the TOE and a Security Objective of the Operational Environment can mitigate a threat. The same can be done for OSPs such as:

P.SSL   The Secure Socket Layer (SSL) communications protocol shall be used to protect transmitted data within the Organization as well as with trusted external IT entities.

The Organizational Security Policy P.SSL can be addressed by OE.SSL and O.SSL.

Assumptions are used to articulate requirement that are solely the responsibility of the Operational Environment. These are typically requirements on non-IT resources such as personnel and physical surroundings. Examples of Assumptions are:

A.PHYSICAL   The TOE components shall be located in a physically secure environment.
A.NOEVIL   The authorized administrators are not careless, willfully negligent, or hostile, and will follow and abide by the instructions provided by the TOE documentation.

73

A.TIME   The TOE has a trusted source for system time via NTP server.

Security Objectives Rationale

The purpose of the Security Objectives Rationale is to satisfy the ASE_OBJ.2.2C – ASE_OBJ.2.6C requirements. These requirements are intended to illustrate that all of the Threats, Organizational Security Policies (OSP), and Assumptions are addressed by the Security Objectives of the TOE and Security Objectives of the Operational Environment. There shall be no extraneous objectives, and no threats or OSPs left uncovered. The easiest way to illustrate this coverage is with a matrix such as the one shown in the example below.

OBJECTIVES / ASSUMPTIONS/ THREATS/ POLICIES	O.CAPTURE_EVENT	O.MANAGE_INCIDENT	O.SEC_ACCESS	OE.TIME	OE.ENV_PROTECT	OE.PERSONNEL	OE.PHYSEC
A.CONFIG						✓	
A.MANAGE						✓	
A.NOEVIL						✓	
A.LOCATION							✓
A.TIME				✓			
T.NO_AUTH		✓			✓	✓	✓
T.NO_PRIV		✓					
P.EVENTS	✓			✓		✓	
P.INCIDENTS		✓		✓		✓	

Table 10 - Example Objectives Mapping

In addition to this visual illustration of the coverage, there needs to be an explanation of how each Objective addresses the Threats, Assumptions, and OSPs. The following provides some examples of the explanations (rationale) for how these are addressed.

74

ASSUMPTION/ THREAT/ POLICY	RATIONALE
A.CONFIG	This assumption is addressed by OE.PERSONNEL, which ensures that the TOE is managed and administered to receive all events from network-attached devices. This objective also ensures that those responsible for the TOE install, manage, and operate the TOE in a secure manner
T.NO_PRIV	This threat is countered by O.SEC_ACCESS, which ensures that the TOE allows access to the security functions, configuration, and associated data only by authorized users and applications.
P.INCIDENTS	This organizational security policy is enforced by O.MANAGE_INCIDENT, which ensures that the TOE will provide the capability to provide case management functionality to manage the resolution of incidents and OE.TIME, which ensures that the TOE operating environment shall provide an accurate timestamp (via reliable NTP server) and OE.PERSONNEL, which ensures that authorized administrators are non-hostile and follow all administrator guidance and ensures that the TOE is delivered, installed, managed, and operated in a manner that maintains the TOE security objectives. Any operator of the TOE must be trusted not to disclose their authentication credentials to any individual not authorized for access to the TOE.

Table 11 - Objective Rationale Examples

Section 5: Extended Components Definition

The Extended Components Definition section of the ST defines any extended (i.e., customized, non-standard) Security Functional Requirements (SFR) that the ST author has chosen to include in the ST. The requirements are stated in the following table.

ASE_ECD.1 Extended components definition

DEVELOPER ACTION ELEMENT	DESCRIPTION
ASE_ECD.1.1D	The developer shall provide a statement of security requirements.
ASE_ECD.1.2D	The developer shall provide an extended components definition.
CONTENT AND PRESENTATION ELEMENTS	DESCRIPTION
ASE_ECD.1.1C	The statement of security requirements shall identify all extended security requirements.
ASE_ECD.1.2C	The extended components definition shall define an extended component for each extended security requirement.
ASE_ECD.1.3C	The extended components definition shall describe how each extended component is related to the existing CC components, families, and classes.
ASE_ECD.1.4C	The extended components definition shall use the existing CC components, families, classes, and methodology as a model for presentation.
ASE_ECD.1.5C	The extended components shall consist of measurable and objective elements such that conformance or nonconformance to these elements can be demonstrated.

Table 12 - ASE_ECD.1 Requirements

The developer action element requirements for ASE_ECD.1 are met by meeting all of the respective content and presentation element requirements.

In Chapter 4: Preparation for the ST, I expressed my view that SFRs should be chosen from those provided in [CC2] rather than defining customized SFRs. However, if there is a justifiable reason for creating specialized SFRs, they must be defined completely in Section 5: Extended Components Definition of the ST. The SFRs must not only be defined in Section 5, there must also be an explanation (rationale) provided for why there is a need to create the Extended Components.

Please note that in this context the terms "component" and "Security Functional Requirement (SFR)" are used synonymously even though the CC standards have different, specific definitions for each.

76

While the CC standards do not specifically limit the use of extended components to Security Functional Requirements (SFRs), I have not seen any instances where this has been used for Security Assurance Requirements (SARs). The discussion that follows will assume that Extended Components will refer to SFRs only. Generally, any "extensions" to SARs are done through augmenting the standard Evaluation Assurance Levels (EALs) rather than creating new SARs.

Definition of Extended Components

Extended Components must be defined and described with as much detail as any of the standard SFRs in [CC2}. The CC standards suggest that these definitions be done in a "similar manner to the existing CC components." I would suggest creating these extended definitions exactly like the standard definitions to avoid confusion and unnecessary comments back from the evaluators and certifiers. There are several parts to the standard definition of an SFR. These parts include:

- Class Identification
- Family Identification and Behavior Description
- Component Leveling
- Management and Audit Requirements
- Hierarchy
- Dependencies
- SFR Component Definition

If the ST claims strict conformance to a Protection Profile (PP), then any extended components defined in the PP should be reproduced exactly into the ST. This is most easily accomplished with copy-and-paste operations from the PP to the ST.

To explain the format and content of the Extended Components Definition section of the ST that satisfy the ASE_ECD.1 requirements, I present a simple example and explain how it meets the requirements. This example defines an extended component called: FDP_AVP_EXT.1: Anti-Virus Protection.

Class: User Data Protection (FDP)

User data protection involves functionality for TOE security functions and TOE security function policies related to protecting user data. The extended component FDP_AVP_EXT_1: Anti-Virus Protection is mod-

77

eled after the CC component FDP_RIP.1: Residual Information Protection.

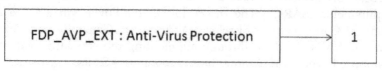

Figure 7 - FDP_AVP_EXT: Anti-Virus Protection Family

Anti-Virus Protection (FDP_AVP_EXT)

Family Behavior:
This family addresses the need to scan for, detect, and take appropriate action against possible computer virus threats.

Component Leveling:

Figure 8 - FDP_AVP_EXT: Anti-Virus Protection Components

FDP_AVP_EXT.1 Anti-Virus Protection requires that the TSF scan for, detect, and take action against possible computer virus threats.

Management: FDP_AVP_EXT.1
The following actions could be considered for the management functions in FMT:
- Configuration of the virus scanning parameters
- Configuration of the virus detection actions

Audit: FDP_AVP_EXT.1
The following actions should be auditable if FAU_GEN Security audit data generation is included in the ST:
- Detection of a computer virus

FDP_AVP_EXT.1 Anti-Virus Protection
Hierarchical to: No other components.
Dependencies: No dependencies.

FDP_AVP_EXT.1.1   The TSF shall scan for computer viruses using [*Assignment: Virus scanning methods*] using the scanning parameters.

78

FDP_AVP_EXT.1.2   The TSF shall take the following actions [*As-signment: Virus detection actions*] based on detection action rules.

The FDP_AVP_EXT.1: Anti-Virus Protection is created as an extended component in the standard Security Functional Class FDP: User Data Protection. ST authors should use existing classes whenever possible to add extended components. Given the long history of CC and the extensive resources devoted to the development of these classes over time, it is highly unlikely that a new class needs to be created. It also saves documentation development effort if you can leverage the standard classes. Creating a new family within an existing class is more commonly done.

The Extended Components Definition must state which standard class is being modelled. The diagram shown (and copied in the Component Leveling section) illustrates the components within the family. In the example, there is only one component.

The FDP_AVP_EXT.1 identifier uses the "_EXT" in accordance with the ST documentation conventions for extended security function components.

The Family Behavior section briefly describes the custom-defined security functions.

The Management requirements for FDP_AVP_EXT.1 include the configuration of scanning parameters and detection actions. SFRs in FMT Security Management must be included in the ST to cover these configuration parameters.

The detection of a potential virus is an auditable event and must be recorded and must be included in the list of auditable events for FAU_GEN.1.

The ST author must be sure that all applicable hierarchical components and dependencies of an extended component are included in the definition of that extended component. Note that a hierarchical component is one whose functionality is subsumed by the "higher" component. For example, Component A requires that the TOE <u>detect</u> a security breach while Component B requires that the TOE <u>detect and react</u> to a security breach. Component B's definition shall state that it is hierarchical to A.

In the example, there are two subcomponents: one that requires scanning using a method determined by the ST author; and one that requires that an action is taken upon detection of a virus. The Assignment clauses are used so that the ST author can describe the option(s) used by the TOE.

Rationale for Extended Components

The ASE_ECD.1.3C requirement states that "The extended components definition shall describe how each extended component is related to the existing CC components, families, and classes." Moreover, the evaluator is given the requirement ASE_ECD.1.2E that states "The evaluator shall confirm that no extended component can be clearly expressed using existing components." This is why we include this rationale in the Extended Components Definition. The rationale that can be given for the FDP_AVP_EXT.1 example is:

The FDP_AVP_EXT family is an extension to the FDP: User Data Protection Security Functional Class to add the Anti-Virus Protection functions. The extended component FDP_AVP_EXT.1 has been created to cover the requirements of computer virus scanning and detection actions. The CC standards (CC Part 2) do not have any components that sufficiently cover this functionality.

Section 6: Security Requirements

The Security Requirements section of the ST describes all of the Security Functional Requirements (SFRs) and all of the Security Assurance Requirements (SARs) that the ST author has chosen to include in the ST. The requirements for this section of the ST are shown in the table below.

ASE_REQ.2 Derived security requirements

DEVELOPER ACTION ELEMENT	DESCRIPTION
ASE_REQ.2.1D	The developer shall provide a statement of security requirements.
ASE_REQ.2.2D	The developer shall provide a security requirements rationale.
CONTENT AND PRESENTATION ELEMENTS	DESCRIPTION

ASE_REQ.2.1C	The statement of security requirements shall describe the SFRs and the SARs.
ASE_REQ.2.2C	All subjects, objects, operations, security attributes, external entities and other terms that are used in the SFRs and the SARs shall be defined.
ASE_REQ.2.3C	The statement of security requirements shall identify all operations on the security requirements.
ASE_REQ.2.4C	All operations shall be performed correctly.
ASE_REQ.2.5C	Each dependency of the security requirements shall either be satisfied, or the security requirements rationale shall justify the dependency not being satisfied.
ASE_REQ.2.6C	The security requirements rationale shall trace each SFR back to the security objectives for the TOE.
ASE_REQ.2.7C	The security requirements rationale shall demonstrate that the SFRs meet all security objectives for the TOE.
ASE_REQ.2.8C	The security requirements rationale shall explain why the SARs were chosen.
ASE_REQ.2.9C	The statement of security requirements shall be internally consistent.

Table 13 - ASE_REQ.2 Requirements

The developer action element requirements for ASE_REQ.2 are met by meeting all of the respective content and presentation element requirements.

Security Functional Requirements

To meet the SFR portions of ASE_REQ.2.1C through ASE_REQ.2.4C, provide each SFR (including extended components) with all of the TOE-specific details (e.g., selections, assignments, and iterations). For example, FCS_COP.1 in [CC2] is defined as:

FCS_COP.1 Cryptographic operation

FCS_COP.1.1 The TSF shall perform [*assignment: list of cryptographic operations*] in accordance with a specified cryptographic

81

algorithm [*assignment: cryptographic algorithm*] and cryptographic key sizes [*assignment: cryptographic key sizes*] that meet the following: [*assignment: list of standards*].

The ST author should fill in the assignment operations with appropriate information relevant to the TOE as shown in the example. Also, note the formatting should be consistent with the document formatting conventions. The Document Formatting Conventions section of the ST explains how the SFR operations (e.g., selection and assignments) are highlighted with underlining and italicized text. This formatting helps evaluators determine if ASE_REQ.2.2C is properly satisfied by making it easier for them to determine where the operation values are. However, I have found that it is important to ensure consistency with those document conventions as it also makes it easier for evaluators to issue comments on simple formatting errors.

FCS_COP.1(1) Cryptographic operation (AES Encryption)

FCS_COP.1.1(1)   The TSF shall perform *encryption and decryption* in accordance with a specified cryptographic algorithm *AES* and cryptographic key sizes *128 and 256 bits* that meet the following: *FIPS PUB 197, "Advanced Encryption Standard (AES)"*

Application Note: AES is used as the encryption method for Transport Layer Security (TLS) communications.

The completed example above shows the iteration operation FCS_COP.1(1) for AES encryption along with an Application Note indicating that AES is used to support TLS communications. The iteration is used because there will be several cryptographic operations supported by the TOE in order to support TLS. The Application Note supplements the TOE Summary Specification (TSS) to help the evaluator recognize what the AES cryptographic operation is used for.

Completing the Security Functional Requirements section of the ST is difficult because it is not always apparent whether the TOE actually meets the requirements of the claimed SFRs and how to properly express the product functionality with the appropriate SFR. Chapter 4: Preparation for the ST provides some insights into the more popular SFRs but completing this section of the ST smoothly and effectively takes experience and is subject to interpretation by the ST author, evaluators, and certifiers.

If the ST claims strict conformance to a Protection Profile (PP), then the SFRs need to be copied exactly from the PP with the appropriate operation values. This is most easily accomplished with copy-and-paste operations from the PP to the ST.

Security Functional Requirements Rationale

Section 3: Security Problem Definition (SPD) of the ST defines the Threats, Assumptions, and Organizational Security Policies (OSP) to be addressed by the TOE and its Operational Environment. Section 4: Security Objectives explains how the Objectives of the TOE and the Objectives of the Operational Environment will address the SPD.

The Security Functional Requirements Rationale section of the ST is intended to covers the ASE_REQ.2.5C – ASE_REQ.2.9C requirements for SFRs and explains how the claimed SFRs will meet the Objectives of the TOE. An effective way to present this explanation is in the following tables:

- SFR-to-Objectives mapping
- Explanation of coverage
- Dependency rationale

Below is a partial example of the SFR-to-Objectives mapping table. At a glance the evaluator can determine how all of the Security Objectives are covered to meet the requirement in ASE_REQ.2.7C.

SFR \ OBJECTIVES	O.CAPTURE_EVENT	O.MANAGE_EVENT	O.SEC_ACCESS
FAU_GEN.1	✓		
FDP_ACC.1			✓
FDP_ACF.1			✓
FIA_UAU.1			✓
FIA_UID.1			✓
FMT_MTD.1		✓	

Table 14 – SFR-to-Objectives Mapping

83

To meet the ASE_REQ.2.8C, the SFR to Objectives Mapping table is augmented by a table similar to the example given below that provides more detail on how each Objective is met by the SFRs.

OBJECTIVE	RATIONALE
O.CAPTURE_EVENT	This objective ensures that the TOE captures security events in an audit log. FAU_GEN.1 defines the auditing capability for incidents and administrative access control and stored in the audit logs.
O.SEC_ACCESS	This objective ensures that the TOE allows access to the security functions, configuration, and associated data only by authorized users and applications. FDP_ACC.1 requires that all management functions for User names, User passwords, and User permissions are controlled. FDP_ACF.1 supports FDP_ACC.1 by ensuring that access to management functions for User names, User passwords, and User permissions is based on the user privilege level and their allowable actions FIA_UID.1 requires the TOE to enforce identification of all users prior to performing TSF-initiated actions on behalf of the user. FIA_UAU.1 requires the TOE to enforce authentication of all users prior to performing TSF-initiated actions on behalf of the user.
O.MANAGE_EVENTS	This objective ensures that the TOE manages security events. FMT_MTD.1 requires the TOE to allow only authorized users to manage TSF data.

Table 15 - Objective Rationale

The Dependency Rationale table is intended to satisfy the ASE_REQ.2.5C requirement. Recall that the dependencies are defined for each SFR by [CC2] or in the Extended Component Definition section of the ST.

SFR	DEPENDENCIES	RATIONALE
FAU_GEN.1	FPT_STM.1	Satisfied by the Operational Environment (OE.TIME)
FDP_ACC.1	FDP_ACF.1	Satisfied by FDP_ACF.1
FDP_ACF.1	FDP_ACC.1 FMT_MSA.3	Satisfied by FDP_ACC.1 and FMT_MSA.3
FIA_UAU.1	FIA_UID.1	Satisfied by FIA_UID.1
FIA_UID.1	N/A	N/A
FMT_MSA.1	FDP_ACC.1 or FDP_IFC.1 and FMT_SMF.1 and FMT_SMR.1	Satisfied by FDP_ACC.1, FMT_SMF.1, and FMT_SMR.1
FMT_MSA.3	FMT_MSA.1 FMT_SMR.1	Satisfied by FMT_MSA.1 and FMT_SMR.1
FMT_SMF.1	N/A	N/A
FMT_SMR.1	FIA_UID.1	Satisfied by FIA_UID.1

Table 16 - Dependency Coverage Map

Security Assurance Requirements

The Security Assurance Requirements section of the ST meets ASE_REQ.2.1C by providing the following tables of SARs and their descriptions based on the selected Evaluation Assurance Level (EAL) as defined in [CC3]. Below are the tables for EAL2 and EAL4. If the ST claims any augmented components (e.g., ALC_FLR.2) those should be listed as well.

ASSURANCE CLASS	COMPONENTS
ASE: Security Target	ASE_INT.1 ST introduction
	ASE_CCL.1 Conformance claims
	ASE_SPD.1 Security problem definition
	ASE_OBJ.2 Security objectives
	ASE_ECD.1 Extended components definition
	ASE_REQ.2 Derived security requirements
	ASE_TSS.1 TOE summary specification
ALC: Life-cycle support	ALC_CMC.2 Use of a CM system
	ALC_CMS.2 Parts of the TOE CM coverage
	ALC_DEL.1 Delivery procedures

ADV: Development	ADV_ARC.1 Security architecture description
	ADV_FSP.2 Security-enforcing functional specification
	ADV_TDS.1 Basic design
AGD: Guidance	AGD_OPE.1 Operational user guidance
	AGD_PRE.1 Preparative procedures
ATE: Tests	ATE_COV.1 Evidence of coverage
	ATE_FUN.1 Functional testing
	ATE_IND.2 Independent testing - sample
AVA: Vulnerability assessment	AVA_VAN.2 Vulnerability analysis

Table 17 - EAL2 Requirements

ASSURANCE CLASS	COMPONENTS
ASE: Security Target	ASE_INT.1 ST introduction
	ASE_CCL.1 Conformance claims
	ASE_SPD.1 Security problem definition
	ASE_OBJ.2 Security objectives
	ASE_ECD.1 Extended components definition
	ASE_REQ.2 Derived security requirements
	ASE_TSS.1 TOE summary specification
ALC: Life-cycle support	ALC_CMC.4 Production support, acceptance procedures and automation
	ALC_CMS.4 Problem tracking CM coverage
	ALC_DEL.1 Delivery procedures
	ALC_DVS.1 Identification of security measures
	ALC_LCD.1 developer defined life-cycle model
	ALC_TAT.1 Well-defined development tools
ADV: Development	ADV_ARC.1 Security architecture description
	ADV_FSP.4 Complete functional specification
	ADV_IMP.1 Implementation representation of the TSF
	ADV_TDS.3 Basic modular design
AGD: Guidance	AGD_OPE.1 Operational user guidance
	AGD_PRE.1 Preparative procedures

ATE: Tests	ATE_COV.2 Analysis of coverage
	ATE_DPT.1 Testing: basic design
	ATE_FUN.1 Functional testing
	ATE_IND.2 Independent testing - sample
AVA: Vulnerability assessment	AVA_VAN.3 Focused vulnerability analysis

Table 18 – EAL4 Requirements

Security Assurance Requirements Rationale

To meet ASE_REQ.2.8C, the Security Assurance Requirements Rationale section of the ST provides the reasons for selecting the given EAL and any augmentation. Generally this requirement can be satisfied with a simple statement such as the one in the example below.

The ST security assurance requirements are from EAL 4 augmented with ALC_FLR.2 – Flaw Reporting Procedures. EAL 4 was selected for this TOE because it reflects good commercial practice expected of this type of TOE. EAL4 is augmented by ALC_FLR.2 to ensure that the customers can report the flaws and the flaws can be systematically corrected.

In addition to the rationale, many STs include a table describing the evidence documents that will be provided to satisfy the assurance requirements. This does not appear to be a written requirement in [CC3] or [CEM] and in part duplicates the content of the Configuration Item (CI) List in the Configuration Management (CM) document (see Chapter 7: Configuration Management for more details on the CI list), but seems to be requested by evaluators. The following is an example of this table of evidence documents for an EAL2 evaluation augmented with ALC_FLR.2.

SECURITY ASSURANCE REQUIREMENT	EVIDENCE TITLE
ADV_ARC.1: Security Architecture Description	Security Architecture: Securitee Inc. Cyber-Sleuth v2.0
ADV_FSP.2: Security-Enforcing Functional Specification	Functional Specification: Securitee Inc. CyberSleuth v2.0
ADV_TDS.1: Basic Design	Basic Design: Securitee Inc. CyberSleuth v2.0

SECURITY ASSURANCE REQUIREMENT	EVIDENCE TITLE
AGD_OPE.1 Operational User Guidance	Securitee Inc. CyberSleuth v2.0Users Guide Operational User Guidance and Preparative Procedures Supplement: Securitee Inc. CyberSleuth v2.0
AGD_PRE.1 Preparative Procedures	Securitee Inc. CyberSleuth v2.0 Setup and Installation Guide Operational User Guidance and Preparative Procedures Supplement: Securitee Inc. CyberSleuth v2.0
ALC_CMC.2: Use of a CM System	Configuration Management Processes and Procedures: Securitee Inc. CyberSleuth v2.0
ALC_CMS.2: Parts of the TOE CM Coverage	Configuration Management Processes and Procedures: Securitee Inc. CyberSleuth v2.0
ALC_DEL.1 Delivery Procedures	Secure Delivery Processes and Procedures: Securitee Inc. CyberSleuth v2.0
ALC_FLR.2: Flaw Reporting	Flaw Remediation Process: Securitee Inc. CyberSleuth v2.0
ATE_COV.1: Evidence of Coverage	Test Plan and Coverage Analysis: Securitee Inc. CyberSleuth v2.0
ATE_FUN.1 Functional Testing	Test Plan and Coverage Analysis: Securitee Inc. CyberSleuth v2.0
ATE_IND.2 Independent Testing - sample	Test Plan and Coverage Analysis: Securitee Inc. CyberSleuth v2.0

Table 19 - Evidence Table

Section 7: TOE Summary Specification

The TOE Summary Specification (TSS) is the narrative version of Section 6: Security Requirements and a more detailed version of the TOE Description in Section 1: ST Introduction of the ST. The TSS describes how requirements in each claimed security functional class are met by the TOE. The TSS is a lead-in to the Functional Specifications document in the ADV: Development assurance class described further in Chapter 15: Functional Specifications which provides very specific details of how the TOE meets the individual Security Functional Requirements (SFRs).

The content requirements for the TSS are summarized in following the table.

ASE_TSS.1 TOE summary specification

DEVELOPER ACTION ELEMENT	DESCRIPTION
ASE_TSS.1.1D	The developer shall provide a TOE summary specification.
CONTENT AND PRESENTATION ELEMENTS	DESCRIPTION
ASE_TSS.1.1C	The TOE summary specification shall describe how the TOE meets each SFR.

Table 20 - ASE_TSS.1 Requirements

The TSS is oftentimes organized by Security Functional Class (SFC) and provides a narrative description for how each SFR within the SFC is met by the TOE. This organization is completely optional but it does make it easier for the evaluator to locate explanations for the TOE functionality. To make it even more apparent to the evaluator how each SFR is addressed, it is helpful to indicate the applicable SFR in the narrative. Below is a simplified example.

Security Audit

The TOE component generates three types of audit logs. These logs are used to store different types of security-relevant events. The three types of logs are:
1) system logs
2) network traffic flow logs
3) network traffic alert logs

Each event log contains the date and time of the event, subject identity, and success or failure of the event. Activity logs including login/logout and system start-up and shutdown are logged in the system log.

The TOE provides a web-based GUI interface to review auditable events. The Administrator is granted the capability to read all audit data generated within the TOE via this interface. The TOE does not provide any means to delete audit records.

The Security Audit function is designed to satisfy the following security functional requirements:
- FAU_GEN.1
- FAU_SAR.1

89

Note that the TSS descriptions should address all of the subcomponents of each SFR. The example explains how FAU_GEN.1.1a, b, and c and FAU_GEN.1.2a and b requirements are met by the TOE.

As I pointed out in Chapter 1: Introduction, the CC evaluation process and evidence document development effort can be quite iterative. The Security Target (ST) document can get updated not only in response to evaluator comments during their review but also as other evidence is produced. As the developer produces other CC documents especially the Development (ADV) documents and the Test Plan (ATE), refinements and corrections to the ST may be necessary. For example, the initial ST may state that the TOE will generate audit logs entries for all user activity. As the Functional Specifications (FSP) document is being written it may be uncovered that only certain user events are logged. The ST will need to be updated to reflect the true capabilities of the TOE. To reduce this type of rework effort, spend more time initially to ensure that the claims made in the initial ST are accurate. This may require digging into the details of the TOE's operations and design.

PART III: LIFECYCLE

This part contains:

Chapter 6: Lifecycle Overview

The Lifecycle Support (ALC) assurance class requirements are intended to provide greater assurance through the documentation of processes and tools used in the development, delivery, and support of the TOE. The ALC class consists of seven families that will be discussed in detail in this part of the book.

- Configuration Management consists of CM capabilities (ALC_CMC), a detailed description of the management of the configuration items; and CM scope (ALC_CMS), a minimum set of configuration items to be managed in the defined way.
- Delivery (ALC_DEL) defines the procedures used for the secure delivery of the TOE to the consumer.
- Lifecycle Definition (ALC_LCD) is the high-level description of the TOE development and maintenance lifecycle.
- Development Security (ALC_DVS) is concerned with the developer's physical, procedural, and personnel security measures used during the development of the TOE.
- Tools and Techniques (ALC_TAT) describes the development tools and implementation standards used by the developer.
- Flaw Remediation (ALC_FLR) explains the handling of security flaws.

The ALC documents are analogous to the evidence documents needed for an ISO 9001 audit. These documents explain the actual processes used in the organization for the purposes of an audit by an independent party. Although the audit reviews are conducted against standard criteria, there are no "right" answers. The ALC documents need to describe in sufficient detail the secure processes used by the developer to convince the evaluator that the descriptions are consistent, clear, and meet the assurance requirements.

The following diagram shows generally how the different ALC documents cover the various phases of the TOE lifecycle.

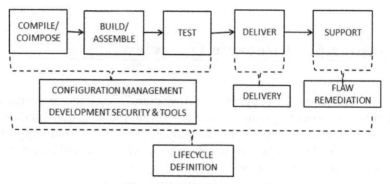

Figure 9 - ALC Documents

The Configuration Management (CM) document describes the use of the CM Plan and CM System during the composition and building of the TOE by the developer. For software TOEs, this will involve describing the use of source code control systems, build and test processes. For TOEs with hardware components, the CM document must describe the list of hardware components and how the assembly process ensures the use of the correct components.

Development Security (DVS) requires a description of the physical, procedural, and personnel measures used by the development staff to ensure the security of the TOE development environment. The Tools and Techniques (TAT) used to ensure the security of the TOE development are oftentimes documented with DVS. DVS and TAT are required for EAL4.

The Delivery (DEL) document describes the process of securely delivering the finished TOE from the developer to their customer. The DEL document describes the roles of any third-parties involved in the delivery process along with the processes they employ.

The Lifecycle Definition (LCD) document is required at EAL4 and is an overview of the entire lifecycle of the TOE from inception to maintenance to end-of-life.

Flaw Remediation (FLR) explains the defect tracking and management processes and tools used by the developer. ALC_FLR.1 or ALC_FLR.2 is oftentimes added to standard EAL packages to augment the evaluation with generally available defect handling procedures.

The ALC requirements differ significantly between EAL2 and EAL4. The following table summarizes the requirements for EAL2 versus EAL4. The details of the requirements will be covered in the other chapters of this part of the book.

94

ALC FAMILY	EAL2	EAL4
Configuration Management	ALC_CMC.2 ALC_CMS.2	ALC_CMC.4 ALC_CMS.4
Delivery	ALC_DEL.1	ALC_DEL.1
Lifecycle Definition	N/A	ALC_LCD.1
Development Security	N/A	ALC_DVS.1
Tools & Techniques	N/A	ALC_TAT.1
Flaw Remediation	ALC_FLR.1 or 2 (Augmentation)	ALC_FLR.1 or 2 (Augmentation)

Table 21 - ALC Family Overview

Note that Flaw Remediation (ALC_FLR) is an augmentation or addition to the standard EAL2 or EAL4 assurance packages. There are no requirements for this family in any standard EAL. Since most commercial developers employ some kind of defect tracking system and can relatively easily document their processes, many opt to augment their evaluations with either ALC_FLR.1 or ALC_FLR.2.

Chapter 7:   Configuration Management

The Configuration Management (CM) assurance requirements are in place to ensure that there is control of the processes for the development and modification of the TOE and related information. CM systems are put in place to ensure the integrity of the TOE by providing mechanisms for tracking changes and by ensuring that all changes are authorized. The objectives are to ensure that the TOE is correct and complete before it is sent to the customer and to prevent unauthorized modification of TOE configuration items. The CM document should present a clear and comprehensive description of these processes. Imagine that a new engineer has joined the product team. He/she should be able to figure out how the CM procedures work based on the descriptions provided in the CM document.

The CM system is required to have capabilities designed to reduce accidental or unauthorized modifications of the configuration items of the TOE. The CM system and processes should ensure the integrity of the TOE from the initial design phases through the maintenance phase.

Automated CM tools are expected to be used to increase the effectiveness of the CM system by helping to reduce human error or negligence.

The CM documentation requirements are broken into two areas:
- CM Capabilities (ALC_CMC)
- CM Scope (ALC_CMS)

In the context of CM, the items that are to be covered by the CM system and procedures are TOE hardware and software, TOE product documentation (e.g., user guides), CC evidence documents, and TOE source code and schematics (e.g., implementation representation).

The CM requirements for EAL4 are more comprehensive than the EAL2 requirements. The two sets of requirements are presented separately in the following sections of this chapter.

EAL2 CM Requirements

The requirements for Configuration Management differ based on EAL. The following tables summarize the CM requirements for EAL2.

ASSURANCE CLASS	COMPONENTS
ALC: Life-cycle support	ALC_CMC.2 Use of a CM system
	ALC_CMS.2 Parts of the TOE CM coverage

Table 22 – CM Requirements – EAL2

ALC_CMC.2 Use of a CM system

DEVELOPER ACTION ELEMENT	DESCRIPTION
ALC_CMC.2.1D	The developer shall provide the TOE and a reference for the TOE.
ALC_CMC.2.2D	The developer shall provide the CM documentation.
ALC_CMC.2.3D	The developer shall use a CM system.
CONTENT AND PRESENTATION ELEMENTS	DESCRIPTION
ALC_CMC.2.1C	The TOE shall be labelled with its unique reference.
ALC_CMC.2.2C	The CM documentation shall describe the method used to uniquely identify the configuration items.
ALC_CMC.2.3C	The CM system shall uniquely identify all configuration items.

Table 23 - ALC_CMC.2 Requirements

ALC_CMS.2 Parts of the TOE CM coverage

DEVELOPER ACTION ELEMENT	DESCRIPTION
ALC_CMS.2.1D	The developer shall provide a configuration list for the TOE.
CONTENT AND PRESENTATION ELEMENTS	DESCRIPTION
ALC_CMS.2.1C	The configuration list shall include the following: the TOE itself; the evaluation evidence required by the SARs; and the parts that comprise the TOE.
ALC_CMS.2.2C	The configuration list shall uniquely identify the configuration items.

ALC_CMS.2.3C	For each TSF relevant configuration item, the configuration list shall indicate the developer of the item.

Table 24 - ALC_CMS.2 Requirements

Most commercial product developers should be able to meet the EAL2 CM requirements without having to change any of their existing processes.

The ALC_CMC.2.1C requirement is addressed by defining a "unique TOE reference." The TOE Reference is the same as that used in the ST Introduction of the Security Target. The TOE Reference must include the appropriate name and version for the TOE. For example:

TOE Reference: Securitee Inc. CyberSleuth v2.0 Build 20140604

Note that the example TOE is a software product that uses a build number to uniquely identify the code within the version 2.0. Some developers will use other version identification notations such as v2.0.1 or v2.0 Service Pack 1. Whatever notation is used by the developer should be used in the TOE Reference however; evaluators seem to want to see a build number regardless.

ALC_CMC.2.2C and ALC_CMC.2.3C requirements refer to Configuration Items (CI). These items include:

- Source code for software
- Binary code for software
- User and CC documentation
- Hardware components list for hardware

The method for uniquely identifying each of these items as well as providing a list of those CIs is required to satisfy ALC_CMC.2.2C and ALC_CMC.2.3C. This means that CC documents shall have unique identifiers (e.g., version numbers or dates). Also note that all of the CC documents (e.g., Security Target and all supporting evidence) are expected to be kept under revision control (i.e., CM System).

If an automated revision control system is used, a common way to illustrate the method used to uniquely identify the TOE source code is to provide a reference to the source code tree branch that contains the relevant source code for the TOE. If the binary code is maintained in the same automated revision control system, then the analogous branch can be referenced for the binary code along with the TOE Reference label.

Note that I've included source code in the Configuration List for EAL2 even though Implementation Representation is a requirement in ALC_CMS.4.1C (at EAL4) because in my experience many evaluators interpret "the TOE itself" (in ALC_CMS.1.1C) to include TOE source code. Note that at EAL2, evaluators do not review the source code.

Some developers may use a different revision control system for their user documentation and CC documentation. If so, then references to where the TOE product documentation and all of the CC-specific documentation are stored shall be provided.

If the TOE contains hardware, the list of hardware components or bill of materials (BOM) must be kept under revision control and each component must be referenced in the CM document. Typically, developers provide the BOM for the TOE as an appendix to the CM document.

The sample Configuration List below illustrates how the ALC_CMS.2 requirements are met. Note that each Unique Identifier includes the item version number and author. The example is only a partial list. For an EAL2 evaluation, all of the documents created to address the ADV, ALC, AGD, and ATE security assurance class requirements shall also be included in the Configuration List.

Because the Configuration List includes the version numbers of the CC documents and that the CC documents get updated in response to comments from the evaluators throughout the evaluation, the Configuration List and the CM document will need to be updated before the end of the evaluation to reflect the final document version numbers. Remember to update the CM document version number as well.

CONFIGURATION ITEM (CI)	UNIQUE IDENTIFIER	DESCRIPTION
TOE Software	Securitee Inc. CyberSleuth v2.0 Build 20140604 Author: Securitee Inc.	The TOE software image
TOE Hardware	Securitee Inc. CyberSleuth v2.0 Appliance Author: Securitee Inc.	These documents serve as the Bills of Material and HW diagrams for each hardware component of the TOE.
TOE Source Code	*Source File Listing:* Securitee Inc. CyberSleuth v2.0 Build 20140604	The source code modules are uniquely referenced in the CM system by directory/sub-

CONFIGURATION ITEM (CI)	UNIQUE IDENTIFIER	DESCRIPTION
	Document Version 1.0 Author: Securitee Inc.	directory, file name, and revision number
Security Target	*Security Target:* Securitee Inc. CyberSleuth v2.0 Document Version 1.1 Author: Securitee Inc.	This document identifies Security Functional Requirements (SFRs) and Security Assurance Requirements (SARs), and describes how the TOE meets require-ments.
Configuration Management	*Configuration Management Processes and Procedures:* Securitee Inc. CyberSleuth v2.0 Document Version 1.0 Author: Securitee Inc.	Securitee Inc. uses the procedures described within this document to identify and maintain the configuration for TOE configuration items.
Operational Guides	*Operational User Guidance and Preparative Procedures Supplement:* Securitee Inc. CyberSleuth v2.0 Document Version 1.0 Author: Securitee Inc. Administrator Guide: Securitee Inc. CyberSleuth v2.0 Document Version 1.0 Author: Securitee Inc. Maintenance Guide: Securitee Inc. CyberSleuth v2.0 Document Version 1.0 Author: Securitee Inc.	These manuals describe how a System Adminis-trator and User config-ure, operate, and maintain the TOE.

Table 25 - CI List

EAL4 CM Requirements

The CM requirements for EAL4 are hierarchical (or incremental) to the EAL2 requirements. The following are the CM requirements for

EAL4. The requirements that are incremental to EAL2 are shown in **bold** in the tables below.

ASSURANCE CLASS	COMPONENTS
ALC: Life-cycle support	ALC_CMC.4 Production support, acceptance procedures and automation
	ALC_CMS.4 Problem tracking CM coverage

Table 26 – CM Requirements – EAL4

ALC_CMC.4 Production support, acceptance procedures and automation

DEVELOPER ACTION ELEMENT	DESCRIPTION
ALC_CMC.4.1D	The developer shall provide the TOE and a reference for the TOE.
ALC_CMC.4.2D	The developer shall provide the CM documentation.
ALC_CMC.4.3D	The developer shall use a CM system.
CONTENT AND PRESENTATION ELEMENTS	**DESCRIPTION**
ALC_CMC.4.1C	The TOE shall be labelled with its unique reference.
ALC_CMC.4.2C	The CM documentation shall describe the method used to uniquely identify the configuration items.
ALC_CMC.4.3C	The CM system shall uniquely identify all configuration items.
ALC_CMC.4.4C	**The CM system shall provide automated measures such that only authorised changes are made to the configuration items.**
ALC_CMC.4.5C	**The CM system shall support the production of the TOE by automated means.**
ALC_CMC.4.6C	**The CM documentation shall include a CM plan.**
ALC_CMC.4.7C	**The CM plan shall describe how the CM system is used for the development of the TOE.**
ALC_CMC.4.8C	**The CM plan shall describe the procedures used to accept modified or newly created configuration items as part of the TOE.**

ALC_CMC.4.9C	The evidence shall demonstrate that all configuration items are being maintained under the CM system.
ALC_CMC.4.10C	The evidence shall demonstrate that the CM system is being operated in accordance with the CM plan.

Table 27 - ALC_CMC.4 Requirements

ALC_CMS.4 Problem tracking CM coverage

DEVELOPER ACTION ELEMENT	DESCRIPTION
ALC_CMS.4.1D	The developer shall provide a configuration list for the TOE.
CONTENT AND PRESENTATION ELEMENTS	DESCRIPTION
ALC_CMS.4.1C	The configuration list shall include the following: the TOE itself; the evaluation evidence required by the SARs; the parts that comprise the TOE; **the implementation representation; and security flaw reports and resolution status.**
ALC_CMS.4.2C	The configuration list shall uniquely identify the configuration items.
ALC_CMS.4.3C	For each TSF relevant configuration item, the configuration list shall indicate the developer of the item.

Table 28 - ALC_CMS.4 Requirements

The major difference between CM requirements for EAL2 and EAL4 is the addition of a description of the CM Plan in ALC_CMC.4. The CM Plan is a description of how the CM System (i.e., the automated CM tool used) and the procedures for authorizing and making changes to the TOE configuration items. This is a narrative description of how the developers use the CM System and how the Configuration Items are protected from unauthorized tampering or inadvertent modifications to the TOE.

To meet the requirements in ALC_CMC.4.4C through ALC_CMC.4.10C the CM Plan should include:

- All of the configuration management activities (e.g. creation, modification or deletion of a configuration item);
- Approach used to uniquely reference TOE versions;
- CM tools used including the tool manufacturer's name, tool version number;
- Operating instructions to ensure the CM tools are used correctly in order to maintain the integrity of the TOE;
- Additional items outside the scope of the Configuration List (e.g., development tools, test scripts) that are under CM control;
- Roles and responsibilities of individuals that may perform operations on individual configuration items with different roles applied to different types of configuration items (e.g. user documentation or source code)) an dhow they are staffed;
- Processes used for change management along with evidence that the process is followed (e.g., screenshots of the CM System in use and audit records);
- Procedures used to ensure that only authorized individuals can make changes to configuration items; and
- Procedures used to ensure that concurrency problems do not occur as a result of simultaneous changes to configuration items.

I have found that some evaluators want information about how and when CM users' access is granted and revoked as part of their evaluation of the ALC_CMC.4.4C requirement. They want to know who is involved in the process (especially revocation) and what triggers that process. Secure procedures here would address threats coming from disgruntled employees.

The "demonstrations" required in ALC_CMC.4.9C and ALC_CMC.4.10C may be achieved by an evaluator visit to the developer's site where he/she can observe the live operation of the CM System in lieu of providing screenshots or other evidence.

The incremental requirement for CM Scope for EAL4 over EAL2 is the inclusion of the implementation representation; and security flaw reports and resolution status in ALC_CMS.4.1C. As noted earlier, the implementation representation is an unarticulated requirement in many EAL2 evaluations. For EAL4, flaw reports need to be maintained under a revision control system and included in the Configuration List.

103

Note that ALC_CMS.4.1C considers security flaw reports and resolution status as parts of the TOE. These items overlap the ALC_FLR.1 Basic Flaw Remediation requirements. This is one reason why developers pursuing EAL4 evaluations can easily augment it with ALC_FLR.1 or 2.

Note that many developers use different revision control systems for the different Configuration Items. They may use Subversion for source code control, a home-grown system to manage the binary code, Documentum for user manuals, and Mozilla's Bugzilla for defect report management. Each of these different systems should be described to cover all of the Configuration Items.

Chapter 8: Delivery

The Delivery document (DEL) is designed to describe the processes used for the secure delivery of the TOE from the developer to the customer. The secure delivery requirements are the same for EAL2 and EAL4 and are described in ALC_DEL.1. The requirements are summarized in the table below.

ALC_DEL.1 Delivery procedures

DEVELOPER ACTION ELEMENT	DESCRIPTION
ALC_DEL.1.1D	The developer shall document and provide procedures for delivery of the TOE or parts of it to the consumer.
ALC_DEL.1.2D	The developer shall use the delivery procedures.
CONTENT AND PRESENTATION ELEMENTS	DESCRIPTION
ALC_DEL.1.1C	The delivery documentation shall describe all procedures that are necessary to maintain security when distributing versions of the TOE to the consumer.

Table 29 - ALC_DEL.1 Requirements

The Delivery document should provide enough details about the delivery process to describe the following:
- Procedures to maintain security during transit.
- Procedures that maintain security when delivering the TOE to the consumer.
- Procedures to identify the proper version of the TOE.
- All phases of delivery from the production environment to the installation environment shall be described.
- Details of the packaging and delivery mechanisms used such as shrink wrapped packaging and electronic downloading off the Internet procedures.
- Techniques used by the developer to ensure that tampering or masquerading can be detected. For hardware,

this may include tamper detection seals such as those used to satisfy the FIPS 140-2 tamper evidence requirements. For software, this may involve the use of digital signatures or checksums on the TOE binaries.

The ALC_DEL.1.2 requirement to demonstrate the use of the documented delivery procedures may be met by an evaluator visit to the developer's site or by the actual delivery of the TOE to the evaluator (acting as a customer).

Every developer has a unique delivery process. Some have multiple delivery mechanisms for the same TOE (e.g., software download and DVD delivery) or for different forms of the TOE (e.g., appliance and virtual appliance). Each of these options that are covered by the evaluated configuration should be described in the Delivery document. Some delivery processes involve third-parties that integrate hardware with software or distribute and ship the TOE to the customer. The role of those third-parties and their practices should be documented. Process flows are more easily explained through the effective use of diagrams. The Delivery document should include diagrams and flow charts to illustrate the different processes used. Below is an example.

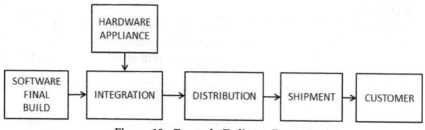

Figure 10 - Example Delivery Process

To explain the above diagram, here is a simplified textual description of the example delivery process.

The developer produces the TOE's software final build. The hardware appliance developed by the developer is integrated with the software by the third-party integrator. The integrator receives the software via a VPN connection to the developer ensuring the integrity of the software. The hardware appliance has a serial number that is communicated securely from the developer to the integrator via a trusted communications channel. The integrator loads the TOE software to the appliance and runs a series of system integrity checks designed to ensure that the

106

correct version of the TOE software has been loaded and that the hardware is operating correctly.

When the integration testing is completed and approved by the QA manager, the appliance is sent to the third-party distribution center. The distribution center and the developer are notified that the unit has moved on to this phase of delivery. The distribution center acts as a warehouse until the unit has been sold to a customer. When the developer receives an order from the customer, a shipping order is sent to the distributor via a trusted communications channel. The shipping order will include the customer name, address, and customer order number.

The distributor uses one of two authorized shipping companies – one for domestic and another for international destinations. Both companies use a tracking mechanism that enables the developer and distributor to track the shipment until receipt is acknowledged by the customer.

The customer verifies delivery by checking the customer order number on the shipping label with the communications sent by the distributor.

My experience has shown that a comprehensive document that describes the end-to-end delivery process should be straight-forward (because developers are able to deliver products to their customers on a daily basis). However, because the delivery process involves so many different departments within the developer's organization and in many cases third-parties, collecting the right information for the Delivery document can be difficult. I've found that no one person understands the complete delivery process so multiple people have to be consulted to get the full picture and all of the necessary details.

For some national Schemes and their certifiers, the use of weak or known-vulnerable hashing algorithms or digital signatures for software verification is unacceptable. MD5 is a popular hashing algorithm used by commercial product developers to detect tampering of binary files however, MD5 is a weak algorithm. Evaluators and certifiers will want to see something stronger used. The strength of even SHA-1 today is questioned.

Another pitfall is the use of third-parties in the delivery process. For many commercial developers using third-parties in the delivery process is a competitive imperative. Developers trust their third-parties because of contractual agreements and confidence developed with experience. That trust does not carry any weight in CC evaluations. The Delivery document must describe how the third-parties protect the TOE during their phases of the delivery process to the same level of detail as any process used by the developer. Sometimes obtaining this detailed information from the third-party is difficult.

108

Chapter 9:   Lifecycle Definition (EAL4)

The idea behind the Lifecycle Definition (LCD) assurance requirement is to show that the developer has a structured, disciplined model for product development, maintenance, and end-of-life. A solid lifecycle model includes the procedures, tools, and techniques used to develop and maintain the TOE. This model may include design methods, review procedures, project management controls, change control procedures, test methods and acceptance procedures. An effective lifecycle model should also include a description of the management structure that assigns responsibilities and monitors progress.

Lifecycle Definition is required for EAL4 (not EAL2). The requirements for ALC_LCD.1 for EAL4 are shown in the following table.

ALC_LCD.1 developer defined life-cycle model

DEVELOPER ACTION ELEMENT	DESCRIPTION
ALC_LCD.1.1D	The developer shall establish a life-cycle model to be used in the development and maintenance of the TOE.
ALC_LCD.1.2D	The developer shall provide life-cycle definition documentation.
CONTENT AND PRESENTATION ELEMENTS	DESCRIPTION
ALC_LCD.1.1C	The life-cycle definition documentation shall describe the model used to develop and maintain the TOE.
ALC_LCD.1.2C	The life-cycle model shall provide for the necessary control over the development and maintenance of the TOE.

Table 30 - ALC_LCD.1 Requirements

The lifecycle model should describe the lifecycle phases of the TOE and the boundaries between the different phases. The different phases may include product inception, design, implementation, test, delivery, maintenance, and end-of-life. This description should include information about the procedures during each phase including control processes, such as feature and defect review sessions and phase exit criteria review.

The model should also describe the tools used during the lifecycle. Some of these tools may overlap the tools required to satisfy the ALC_TAT.1 Tools and Techniques requirements. These are the tools used for design, coding, testing, defect tracking, bug-fixing, and project management.

To demonstrate control over the lifecycle processes, there should be a description of the overall management structure overseeing the implementation of the lifecycle. Individual roles and responsibilities for each of the procedures should be included.

Any participation by third-parties (e.g., subcontractors) should be documented identifying their roles and contributions to the lifecycle process of developing, delivering, or maintaining the TOE.

The purpose of the lifecycle model is to provide assurance that the development and maintenance procedures used reduce the likelihood of security flaws. For example, the life-cycle model should describe the defect review process and provide a means to track the changes to the TOE due to correcting defects. The lifecycle model should have sufficient detail so that the evaluator can determine that solid commercial development practices are in place to mitigate potential security flaws in the TOE.

Below is an example outline of a lifecycle model document.

1. Life-Cycle Model
2. Model Overview
3. Release Team Members
4. Phase 1: Rough Prioritization of Features
   a. Objectives
   b. Exit Goal
5. Phase 2: Write the Product Requirements
   a. Objectives
   b. Overview
   c. Exit Goal
6. Phase 3: Functional Specifications
   a. Objectives
   b. Overview
   c. Exit Goal
7. Phase 4: Test Plan Development
   a. Objectives
   b. Overview
   c. Exit Goal
8. Phase 5: Implementation

The CC standards [CEM] proclaims that the "CC does not mandate any particular development approach, and each should be judged on merit." However, rapid prototyping development methods such as Agile or Scrum may be a bit more difficult to explain the control mechanisms (in ALC_LCD.1.2C) to evaluators. The traditional waterfall development approach employs clear phase exit criteria and review procedures. This makes it easier for the evaluator to see how the controls are applied. Developers who use Agile development techniques may have to make special efforts to explain their analogous control mechanisms.

Chapter 10: Development Security and Tools (EAL4)

This chapter covers the requirements for Development Security (ALC_DVS.1) and Tools and Techniques (ALC_TAT.1) that are required for EAL4 evaluations. For simplicity, the document is called the Development Security (DVS) document. These two assurance family requirements are discussed together because they can conveniently be described in a single document. Development Security covers the physical, procedural, personnel, and other security measures used in the development environment to protect the TOE and its components. Tools and Techniques deals with the tools that are used to securely develop, analyze, and implement the TOE.

The requirements for ALC_DVS.1 and ALC_TAT.1 are summarized in the following tables.

ALC_DVS.1 Identification of security measures

DEVELOPER ACTION ELEMENT	DESCRIPTION
ALC_DVS.1.1D	The developer shall produce and provide development security documentation.
CONTENT AND PRESENTATION ELEMENTS	DESCRIPTION
ALC_DVS.1.1C	The development security documentation shall describe all the physical, procedural, personnel, and other security measures that are necessary to protect the confidentiality and integrity of the TOE design and implementation in its development environment.

Table 31 - ALC_DVS.1 Requirements

ALC_TAT.1 Well-defined development tools

DEVELOPER ACTION ELEMENT	DESCRIPTION
ALC_TAT.1.1D	The developer shall provide the documentation identifying each development tool being used for the TOE.
ALC_TAT.1.2D	The developer shall document and provide the selected implementation dependent options of each development tool.
CONTENT AND PRESENTATION ELEMENTS	DESCRIPTION
ALC_TAT.1.1C	Each development tool used for implementation shall be well-defined.
ALC_TAT.1.2C	The documentation of each development tool shall unambiguously define the meaning of all statements as well as all conventions and directives used in the implementation.
ALC_TAT.1.3C	The documentation of each development tool shall unambiguously define the meaning of all implementation-dependent options.

Table 32 - ALC_TAT.1 Requirements

Development Security

The Development Security (DVS) document should be comprised of the following sections:

- Physical Security Measures
- Procedural Security Measures
- Personnel Security Measures
- Other Security Measures

Physical Security Measures

The physical protection of the TOE development environment should limit physical access to the facility that houses the TOE development environment. A typical measure taken by commercial product developers is to only allow access to personnel who have been authenti-

113

cated using electronic card keys issued by the developer's management staff.

Procedural Security Measures

Procedural security measures are instituted by the organization to augment tools used to protect the TOE development environment. Many commercial developers limit visitor access to their development sites by requiring the visitors to sign-in and wear visitor badges before being granted escorted access to the buildings. Procedures for compartmentalizing sensitive information are also employed to reduce the risk of exposure to unauthorized personnel as well as procedures for disposing of sensitive information.

Personnel Security Measures

Personnel security measures should instill trust in the developers of the TOE. These measures may include descriptions of the new hire vetting and screening process. It may also cover the privilege revocation process for developers who are terminated or no longer associated with the development of the TOE. These personnel can include contractors as well as regular employees.

Other Security Measures

The DVS document may also discuss other security measures such as the physical or logical separation of TOE source code from other products to prevent inadvertent "data leakage" across products. It may also discuss how access to TOE sensitive information by remote employees is protected by the use of Virtual Private Networks (VPN) or other protocols. Tool configurations or user permissions that restrict access to networks or systems may also be included in the DVS descriptions.

Tools and Techniques

The tools used by the developer to develop, test, and maintain the TOE may be mentioned in other CC evidence documents (e.g., Configuration Management or Flaw Remediation) but the Tools and Techniques (TAT) requires that more detail be provided for those tools and others. To satisfy the ALC_TAT.1 requirements the following information should be provided for each tool.

- Tool name
- Tool version
- Tool vendor
- Purpose and use of the tool
- References to tool guides

A table is sufficient to satisfy the ALC_TAT.1 requirements. An example of a tabular form for TAT is shown below. Note that the references point to the online user guides for the tools which provide all of the details for the correct operation of the tools and an explanation for all of the terms used by the tool.

TOOL IDENTIFIER	PURPOSE	REFERENCE
gcc 4.1.1	C and C++ language compiler	http://gcc.gnu.org/onlinedocs/
Visual Studio 2005	Microsoft development suite used to compile source code	http://msdn.microsoft.com/library/ms269115.aspx
Bugzilla version 4.4.4	Defect tracking system	http://www.bugzilla.org/docs/
Perforce version 2010.2/295045	Software source code control system	http://www.perforce.com/documentation/perforce_technical_documentation

Table 33 - Tools Example

Chapter 11: Flaw Remediation (+)

Flaw Remediation (FLR) is more commonly called defect tracking or bug tracking. The ALC_FLR assurance family is not a requirement for any Evaluation Assurance Level (EAL) but because defect tracking is something most commercial developers do, the effort required to produce the FLR documentation is minimal. In some cases, to address customer support or quality requirements, developers already have documentation explaining their defect tracking process. If this documentation describes how security flaws are handled, then it can be used to address the FLR requirements.

Adding FLR to a standard EAL package is called augmenting the EAL is oftentimes denoted with a "+" after the EAL number. For example, augmenting an EAL2 package with ALC_FLR.1 will be denoted EAL2+ or EAL2 Augmented with ALC_FLR.1.

Typically ALC_FLR.1 or ALC_FLR.2 is claimed by commercial developers as the requirements reflect common commercial practice. Both sets of requirements are summarized below. The incremental differences between the ALC_FLR.2 requirements over the ALC_FLR.1 requirements are highlighted in **bold-faced type**.

ALC_FLR.1 Basic flaw remediation

DEVELOPER ACTION ELEMENT	DESCRIPTION
ALC_FLR.1.1D	The developer shall document and provide flaw remediation procedures addressed to TOE developers.
CONTENT AND PRESENTATION ELEMENTS	DESCRIPTION
ALC_FLR.1.1C	The flaw remediation procedures documentation shall describe the procedures used to track all reported security flaws in each release of the TOE.

ALC_FLR.1.2C	The flaw remediation procedures shall require that a description of the nature and effect of each security flaw be provided, as well as the status of finding a correction to that flaw.
ALC_FLR.1.3C	The flaw remediation procedures shall require that corrective actions be identified for each of the security flaws.
ALC_FLR.1.4C	The flaw remediation procedures documentation shall describe the methods used to provide flaw information, corrections and guidance on corrective actions to TOE users.

Table 34 - ALC_FLR.1 Requirements

ALC_FLR.2 Flaw reporting procedures

DEVELOPER ACTION ELEMENT	DESCRIPTION
ALC_FLR.2.1D	The developer shall document and provide flaw remediation procedures addressed to TOE developers.
ALC_FLR.2.2D	**The developer shall establish a procedure for accepting and acting upon all reports of security flaws and requests for corrections to those flaws.**
ALC_FLR.2.3D	**The developer shall provide flaw remediation guidance addressed to TOE users.**
CONTENT AND PRESENTATION ELEMENTS	DESCRIPTION
ALC_FLR.2.1C	The flaw remediation procedures documentation shall describe the procedures used to track all reported security flaws in each release of the TOE.
ALC_FLR.2.2C	The flaw remediation procedures shall require that a description of the nature and effect of each security flaw be provided, as well as the status of finding a correction to that flaw.
ALC_FLR.2.3C	The flaw remediation procedures shall require that corrective actions be identified for each of the security flaws.

ALC_FLR.2.4C	The flaw remediation procedures documentation shall describe the methods used to provide flaw information, corrections and guidance on corrective actions to TOE users.
ALC_FLR.2.5C	**The flaw remediation procedures shall describe a means by which the developer receives from TOE users reports and enquiries of suspected security flaws in the TOE.**
ALC_FLR.2.6C	**The procedures for processing reported security flaws shall ensure that any reported flaws are remediated and the remediation procedures issued to TOE users.**
ALC_FLR.2.7C	**The procedures for processing reported security flaws shall provide safeguards that any corrections to these security flaws do not introduce any new flaws.**
ALC_FLR.2.8C	**The flaw remediation guidance shall describe a means by which TOE users report to the developer any suspected security flaws in the TOE.**

Table 35 - ALC_FLR.2 Requirements

Even if a developer has documentation describing their defect tracking system and procedures, if the system and processes do not differentiate security issues from other defects, it will not be acceptable on its own to satisfy the FLR requirements. That is because the requirements call for the tracking of security flaws. There needs to be some way to differentiate security flaws from other product flaws. Moreover, many evaluators will insist that security flaws should be treated differently (i.e., with higher priority) even if the CC standards do not explicitly call for it.

Like the descriptions in the Delivery document (DEL), the FLR should cover the end-to-end process for the lifecycle of the defect report. The following topics would be expected to be covered in the FLR document.

- Defect handling workflow
- Defect tracking tools and versions
- Personnel roles and responsibilities
- Decision processes and criteria
- Defect prioritization and criteria

118

Diagrams and process flow charts are useful in explaining the defect tracking process flows. An example flow chart is provided below.

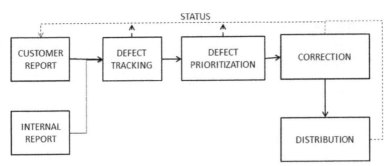

Figure 11 - Defect Tracking Flow

The FLR document should describe in detail each block in the diagram. It should describe how customers (or internal personnel) report defects, what information they provide, and what tools are used.

In most defect tracking mechanisms, there is some analysis and prioritization activity to verify the defect and then assign a priority and/or severity to the defect. The decision process should be described along with who is involved in the decision making process.

The defect correction (patching) phase may be dependent upon the support level provided to the customer. Sometimes patches and hotfixes are made available to "higher-tiered support" customers before others or through special mechanisms. These mechanisms shall all be described. Also the process used to address (publicly disclosed) security vulnerabilities should be described.

The FLR should describe how the customer receives status about the defect reports throughout the process including how the defect resolution (remediation) will be distributed to the customers.

The major differences between ALC_FLR.1 and ALC_FLR.2 are:

- ALC_FLR.2.6C requires that the procedures used to handle defect reports from internal users as well as customers is described, and
- ALC_FLR.2.7C requires a description of the procedures used to prevent the introduction of new defects while fixing others.

119

Chapter 12: Site Visit

Evaluators will conduct site visits to verify the Lifecycle processes and occasionally observe developer testing and conduct independent testing. The evaluators will verify the actual use of configuration management tools and processes against the CM documentation. The delivery process will be checked against the DEL document. DVS and LCD documents will be verified for EAL4 evaluations. Defect tracking procedures will be checked for those evaluations claiming the ALC_FLR augmentation.

In my experience, evaluators may decide not to conduct a site visit for EAL2 evaluations. They will if there is any question about how any of the lifecycle processes work. At EAL4, a site visit is mandatory. Because EAL4 includes ADV_IMP.1 (Implementation Representation) which oftentimes consists of some source code review and review of other highly-sensitive implementation information, the developer may desire that the evaluator conduct such reviews in the secure confines of the developer's facilities.

Oftentimes, evaluators will provide the developer with a preparatory checklist so that the logistics can be arranged and appropriate personnel can be made available. Developers should ask for this list prior to the site visit to ensure everyone is properly prepared and there is little wasted time. Below is a sample of an outline for this checklist.

1. Purpose of the site visit
2. Assumptions and prerequisites for the site visit
3. Required documentation
4. Agenda for the site visit
5. Logistics
6. Lifecycle Support – Configuration Management
7. Lifecycle Support – Delivery Procedures
8. Lifecycle Support – Development Security
9. Lifecycle Support – Lifecycle Definition
10. Lifecycle Support – Tools and Techniques
11. Lifecycle Support – Flaw Remediation
12. Testing – Independent Testing

The checklists may contain details about what items of interest the evaluator will be checking and verifying. The evaluator may provide advance information on specific requirements (as defined by [CC3] and [CEM]) that will be examined during the site visit.

The evaluator's primary job during the site visit is to verify that the documented procedures are being followed by the developer. The evaluator will check to see how the configuration management system is actually used and what items are actually controlled by that system. The tools used for secure development and defect tracking will be checked including the version numbers of the tools. The documented procedures will be checked for consistency with reality.

It is important to make sure the appropriate developer personnel are available to demonstrate procedures to the evaluator. An accurate agenda and time schedule becomes an important factor here. For example, if a support or quality assurance (QA) engineer is needed to demonstrate the defect tracking system, that person should be made available when the evaluator is ready to verify the FLR document.

If the TOE development is distributed across multiple sites, the evaluator may need to visit all of the key development sites. This requires additional planning, coordination, and cost.

Similarly, if the evaluator will be performing the independent testing during the site visit, the equipment and personnel necessary to execute these tests should be ready. Evaluators may conduct their independent testing at the developer's facilities because the TOE and Operational Environment may require specialized equipment or specific expertise to establish an appropriate test bed.

PART IV: DEVELOPMENT

This part contains:

Chapter 13: Development Overview

The Development (ADV) assurance class of requirements covers the TOE's internal technical design. Where the Lifecycle Support (ALC) documents describe the processes the TOE goes through during the development process, the ADV documents describe the inner workings of the TOE and how it implements the Security Functional Requirements (SFRs).

The ADV requirements clearly reflect the higher assurance provided by the different EALs. The ADV requirements for EAL4 are much more stringent and require significantly more detailed documentation than those for EAL2. Consequently, a lot more effort is required to produce the ADV documentation for EAL4. This issue is compounded by the fact that precious time from technical subject matter experts (SME) are required to provide the detailed information needed to satisfy the documentation requirements.

The table below summarizes the ADV requirements for the 4 assurance families in the ADV class for EAL2 and EAL4.

ADV FAMILY	EAL2	EAL4
Security Architecture	ADV_ARC.1	ADV_ARC.1
Functional Specifications	ADV_FSP.2	ADV_FSP.4
TOE Design	ADV_TDS.1	ADV_TDS.3
Implementation Representation	N/A	ADV_IMP.1

Table 36 - ADV Family Overview

Security Architecture

The Common Criteria standard underwent a significant change when version 2.3 transitioned to version 3.1 in 2006. In that transition, some version 2.3 concepts didn't fall into the new SFRs or SARs. The Security Architecture (ARC) requirements were created to capture the orphaned concepts of secure initialization, non-bypassability, tamper protection, and security domains.

Although the Security Architecture (ARC) requirement (ADV_ARC.1) is the same for both EAL2 and EAL4, the detailed requirement ADV_ARC.1.1C states that the "description shall be at a level of detail commensurate with the description of the SFR-enforcing abstractions described in the TOE design document." This means that since the TOE Design document (TDS) describes the TOE at the subsystem level for EAL2, then the ARC must describe the architecture in terms of subsystems. At EAL4, the TDS describes the TOE at the module level, thus the ARC must be described using modules. Module descriptions require more effort than subsystem descriptions, thus the ARC for EAL4 requires more effort to produce than for EAL2.

Functional Specifications

The Functional Specifications (FSP) requirements treat the TOE as a "black box." The FSP document is required to describe the external interfaces to the TOE. These external interface descriptions must include the purpose of the interface, the parameters used, the error messages generated, and the actions the interface performs.

The FSP requirements differ in breadth of coverage of the interfaces between EAL2 (ADV_FSP.2) and EAL4 (ADV_FSP.4). Where EAL2 only requires that the FSP document the "SFR-enforcing" TOE Security Function Interfaces (TSFI), EAL4 requires that SFR-enforcing, SFR-supporting, and SFR-non-interfering TSFI are described. Thus, the EAL4 FSP is a superset of the EAL2 FSP.

TOE Design

Like the FSP, the TOE Design (TDS) requirements at EAL4 are a superset of the requirements at EAL2. EAL2 requires that the TDS document describes the TOE in terms of "subsystems." Subsystems are a high-level decomposition of the TOE (logical) security functionality. Subsystems are further decomposed into "modules" and described in the TDS for EAL4. Modules are closer to the actual (physical) implementation and are more detailed than subsystems.

These same subsystems and modules described in the TDS shall be consistent with the subsystems and modules described in the Security Architecture (ARC) document.

The TOE Design document will use the same TSFI described in the FSP and provide more detail about the actions the subsystems and modules take once data has been provided from those interfaces. The TDS provides the detailed explanation for how the TOE performs its security functions.

126

The TDS also describes the internal interfaces between subsystems and modules.

The TDS requires the greatest time investment from technical subject matter experts of all the CC documents. It requires deep understanding (especially for EAL4) of the internal designs and implementation of the TOE.

Implementation Representation

Hardware designs and integrated circuit (IC) design language code and software source code are examples of Implementation Representations (IR) of the TOE. The IR must reflect the interfaces described in the FSP and TDS. The subsystem and module functionality described in the TDS must be supported by the IR during code reviews.

Implementation Representation is required for EAL4 (ADV_IMP.1). The only real documentation required for ADV_IMP.1 is the software source code and/or hardware designs and an explanation to the evaluator on how the TOE design descriptions (in the FSP and TDS) map to the actual implementation. Since only a sampling of the IR is required, the mapping may take the form of simple verbal or written instructions from the developer to the evaluator.

Development Document Creation Process

In Chapter 4: Preparation for the ST, I presented my process for creating the Security Target (ST) and its constituent sections including the TOE Overview, Security Requirements, and TOE Summary Specifications (TSS). This process involves gathering information about candidate security functions that are relevant to Common Criteria (CC) evaluations from product documentation and the product itself and including them in the ST. The inner workings (i.e., design) of these security functions are then explained in the Development (ADV) documents. The following is an illustration of this flow of information.

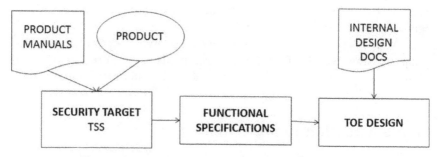

Figure 12 - Development Document Creation Process

User documentation and product demonstrations can be used to illustrate the security functions of the product. The TSS in the ST describes the TOE security functions in fairly plain language (as opposed to the CC language of SFRs). The Functional Specifications (FSP) extends the TSS descriptions by documenting the external interfaces (or TSFI) to the TOE that invoke the security functions. The FSP treats the TOE as a "black box."

An example of a TSFI is the user console. FIA_UID.1 and FIA_UAU.1 are SFRs in the Identification and Authentication class that ensure that users may not have access to any TOE functions without first being successfully identified and authenticated. The applicable external interface or TOE Security Function Interface (TSFI) is the user console where users enter their login credentials. The FSP documents the user console as a TSFI. The details of that TSFI can be found in user manuals and can be referenced in the FSP.

The TOE Design document (TDS) treats the TOE as a "white box." Where the FSP provides a high-level description of the security functions, the TDS provides the details of how the TOE meets the SFRs by explaining the TOE's inner design. The detailed design information can be obtained by examining the product's design documentation, consulting with the developer's technical experts, and occasionally reviewing software source code.

The ST, FSP, and TDS must be:

- Complete - all of the SFRs are covered,
- Consistent - naming is the same across the documents, and
- Accurate – the TOE must implement the features as documented.

128

Chapter 14: Security Architecture describes how to create the Security Architecture document and its unique role in the ADV class of documents. Chapter 18: Implementation Representation (EAL4) describes how the evaluator uses the implementation representation to verify the information presented in all of the ADV documents.

Chapter 14: Security Architecture

The Security Architecture (ARC) document is a catch-all for some security concepts orphaned in the transition from CC version 2.3 to CC version 3.1. These topics are not covered naturally as Security Functional Requirements (SFRs) or Security Assurance Requirements (SARs). The ARC covers the following specific topics:
1. TOE Architecture
2. Security Domains
3. Secure Initialization
4. Tamper Protection
5. Non-Bypassability

The simplest organization of the ARC document is to present each topic in a separate section to address the assurance requirements summarized in the table below. I have found that some of the material may be redundant but this organization makes it easier for the evaluator to find the key information.

ADV_ARC.1 Security architecture description

DEVELOPER ACTION ELEMENT	DESCRIPTION
ADV_ARC.1.1D	The developer shall design and implement the TOE so that the security features of the TSF cannot be bypassed.
ADV_ARC.1.2D	The developer shall design and implement the TSF so that it is able to protect itself from tampering by untrusted active entities.
ADV_ARC.1.3D	The developer shall provide a security architecture description of the TSF.
CONTENT AND PRESENTATION ELEMENTS	DESCRIPTION
ADV_ARC.1.1C	The security architecture description shall be at a level of detail commensurate with the description of the SFR-enforcing abstractions described in the TOE design document.

ADV_ARC.1.2C	The security architecture description shall describe the security domains maintained by the TSF consistently with the SFRs.
ADV_ARC.1.3C	The security architecture description shall describe how the TSF initialisation process is secure.
ADV_ARC.1.4C	The security architecture description shall demonstrate that the TSF protects itself from tampering.
ADV_ARC.1.5C	The security architecture description shall demonstrate that the TSF prevents bypass of the SFR-enforcing functionality.

Table 37 - ADV_ARC.1 Requirements

Security Architecture

Requirement ADV_ARC.1.1C states that the security architecture description shall be commensurate with the level of detail provided in the TOE Design (TDS) document. What this means is that at EAL2, the security architecture description must be in terms of subsystems. For EAL4, the description must be in terms of modules. Chapter 16: Basic Design (EAL2) and Chapter 17: Modular Design (EAL4) will go into more detail about how to define subsystems and modules. It is important that the Security Architecture (ARC) document is consistent with the TDS. For example, the names of the subsystems and modules used in the TDS must be the same ones used in ARC.

To satisfy the ADV_ARC.1.1C requirement, there should be physical architecture and logical (security) architecture descriptions. The contents of the ST Introduction and the TDS can be leveraged to complete this portion of ARC. The goal is to give the evaluator a sense that the TOE has a cohesive security architecture. Here are a few example statements that can explain the security architecture of a TOE.

The TOE is composed of several models of custom-built hardware appliances with an embedded operating system and application software. The operating system interfaces directly with the storage devices and network interfaces. The TOE software works with the operating system to provide all of the security functionality. The hardware models include ...

The security appliance attaches to a physical network that has been separated into zones through port interfaces. Protection of the TOE from

131

physical tampering is ensured by the physical security assumption claimed in the ST (A.PHYSEC). It is assumed that the TOE will remain attached to the physical connections made by an administrator so that the TSF maintains connectivity and cannot be bypassed.

The only remote access allowed is through an HTTPS connection provided by the communications subsystem in the TOE server. The TOE requires that all users identify and authenticate themselves before being allowed access to TOE data or functions. Once users have successfully identified and authenticated with the server, they are only allowed access to functions and data set by administrator-defined permissions. User activity such as login, logout, modifications to parameters, and audit log review are logged by the audit subsystem.

The description of how the subsystems/modules contribute to the security architecture shall also be included in ARC. Below is an example. This same information can be provided in a table that shows the breakdown of the TOE into subsystems and modules (for EAL4) and how each component contributes to the security of the TOE (e.g., SFR enforcement or support).

The TOE is made up of the following subsystems:

SUBSYSTEM	DESCRIPTION
Audit	Enforces the Security Audit SFRs by capturing all of the security events produced by the other modules in the TOE. Also provides the audit review capabilities.
Communications	Enforces the Trusted Path/Channel SFRs and uses the network interfaces to communicate to external IT entities. It relies on a cryptographic module in the subsystem to provide cryptographic functions to protect the communications paths.
Authentication	Enforces the Identification and Authentication SFRs by checking user credentials before allowing access to the TOE functions and data. It also enforces the user permissions set by the administrator.
Management	Enforces the Security Management SFRs including user accounts and policy settings.

The Security Architecture document is intended to take a more global view of the security of the TOE and its Operational Environment. The Security Target explains the individual objectives and SFRs of the TOE, but lacks the overarching view that the ARC is intended to provide.

Security Domains

Security Domains are resources or interfaces provided by the TOE that may be used by malicious entities. The claimed SFRs described in the ST are intended to mitigate the threats from these malicious entities. ADV_ARC.1.2C requires that all security domains be described in terms of all of the claimed SFRs.

Included in this discussion is the notion of domain separation. Domain separation is a property a security domain is created by the TOE for each untrusted active entity to operate on its resources, and then prevents those domains from interfering with one another.

Here is an example of an explanation of the Security Domains and domain separation through the enforcement of the SFRs.

The Client software is installed on general purpose computer (GPC) systems provided by the Operational Environment. The Client retrieves user identification information from the identity server and forwards it to the Server which uses it to enforce security policies. The Operational Environment tis responsible for the correct operation of the underlying GPC's operating system (OE.OS_PROTECT). The communications between the Client and the identity server is protected by the Operational Environment (OE.COMMS).

The Server is composed of the subsystems and modules (see TDS for more details). These subsystems and modules cooperate to form a single security domain which protects the TOE security functions from external interference and tampering.

All network traffic is routed through the Server Once network traffic is received on a Server network port, it is always subject to the security policy rules. All packets arrive at a network port through the Kernel module and are processed by the Policy Enforcement module in the Data Plane subsystem.

Security Domains may be seen as the physical components that comprise the TOE and TOE platforms as these are commonly the source of exposure to malicious entities.

Secure Initialization

The Secure Initialization section of ARC (to satisfy ADV_ARC.1.3C) simply answers the question "How can I trust that the TOE starts up securely?" Once the TOE has been delivered and installed according to the Secure Delivery (DEL) instructions, describe the measures that the TOE takes to ensure that it starts up properly and securely. This should include the boot-up sequence for the software with details on how this sequence prevents tampering. Any power-on self-tests that test the integrity of the hardware and software should also be described. If FPT_TST.1 – Self-Tests is claimed, the details for the implementation of that SFR should be used here. The following is an example of a secure initialization sequence.

The boot sequence of the TOE appliances aids in establishing the security domains and preventing tampering or bypass of security functionality. The following steps are the boot sequence for the TOE:
1. Execute BIOS hardware and memory checks
2. Load and initialize the operating system kernel
3. Execute FIPS 140-2 power-on self-tests
4. Execute software integrity tests
5. Mount the file system
6. Set up network cards to communicate on the network.
7. Start Internet service and routing protocol processes
8. Initialize routing and forwarding tables
9. Activate physical interfaces
10. Load policies. The TOE does not process any network packets until after the policies are successfully loaded.

The description of the initialization sequence can be augmented with explanations of how these steps ensure a secure start-up. This may entail including details of the individual steps and what happens if a step fails.

Tamper Protection

Arguably, the descriptions of tamper protection (and non-bypassability) could be included with the descriptions of the TOE's security architecture but having a separate tamper protection discussion makes it easier for the evaluator to determine how the ADV_ARC.1.4C is satisfied. This section will describe how the TOE protects itself from manipulation from malicious external entities. The description of the tamper protection mechanisms should be comprised of explanations of the SFRs from the Protection of the TSF (FPT) in particular, other SFRs, and Assumptions and Objectives of the Operational Environment. Here is an example of a discussion of tamper protection.

The Client software is installed on Windows PC systems used only for the administrator console in accordance with the assumption in in the ST (A.CONSOLE_ONLY). The operational environment is responsible for protecting the PC operating system and managing access to the system. The TOE protects its management functions by isolating them through authentication (FIA_UID.1, FIA_UAU.1). Once administrators log in with the correct credentials, they are limited to commands in which they have the privileges (FIA_ATD.1). In addition, the communication path is protected against modification and disclosure using TLS and public key certificate authentication (FTP_TRP.1).

The OpenSSL module (in the Control Plane subsystem) provides encryption functions for the communications between the TSF and an administrator through the use of an administrator-initiated HTTPS session using public key certificate based authentication (FCS_COP.1). Assured identification is guaranteed by using public key certificate based authentication for TLS. The TLS protocol ensures that the data transmitted over HTTPS session cannot be disclosed or altered (FTP_TRP.1). This protocol provides encryption and integrity of the transmitted data and makes use of the FIPS 140-2 validated cryptographic module.

The Policy Enforcement module within the Control Plane subsystem allows only packets that meet policy enforcement rules to flow through the Server (FDP_IFC.1). The policy rules enforced are applied to every packet arriving at the Server. ...

The Server bootup sequence includes system integrity checks (FPT_TST.1) and cryptographic module power-on self-tests. If any of these tests fails, the Server goes into a failure state, logs the event, and requires that an administrator take corrective action.

Non-Bypassability

Non-bypassability is the property that the security functionality of the claimed SFRs is always invoked. To properly address the ADV_ARC.1.5C requirement, the description must clearly show how the SFR-enforcing mechanisms cannot be bypassed. For example, if there is an SFR claiming that access controls (e.g., FDP_ACC.1) are in place to protect resources, then there must not be any interfaces that allow access to those resources without invoking the access control mechanisms. As shown in the example below, these descriptions will usually include statements about SFRs and the Assumptions and Objectives of the Operational Environment.

It is assumed that the administrator is trustworthy and configures the Client to only connect to a identity server (A.TRUST_ID). The Client software requires that the administrator who configures the Client must be a member of the trusted admin group on the PC (A.TRUST_ADMIN). The Operational Environment is responsible for managing the access to the Windows operating system (O.TRUST_OS). All network traffic is assumed to be routed through the Server (A.NETWORK). Once network traffic is received on one network interface port, the design of the Server ensures that the network packets are subject to policy enforcement (FDP_IFC.1). ...

All of the interfaces to the appliance are documented in [FSP]. These interfaces do not provide a mode or operation for bypassing the TSF. As required by A.NO_TOE_BYPASS, information cannot flow among the internal and external networks unless it passes through the appliance. In addition, as required by A.PHYSICAL, the appliance will be located within a physically secure, controlled access facility.

Chapter 15:   Functional Specifications

The first thing to note with the CC Functional Specifications (FSP) document is that it is nothing like the functional specifications used in commercial product development. Product functional specifications usually describe how individual product features behave. The purpose of the FSP is to describe the external interfaces to the TOE. The TOE becomes a "black box" (as illustrated in the figure below) in the FSP. The descriptions provided include the purpose, method of use, input parameters, and output errors of the security-relevant interfaces to the TOE. These interfaces are called TOE Security Function Interfaces (TSFIs). The TSFI consists of all means by which external entities supply data to, receive data from, and invoke services from the TOE. It does not describe how the TOE processes service requests; that is addressed by the TOE Design (TDS).

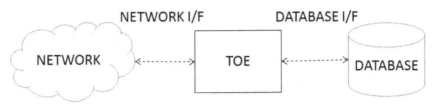

Figure 13 - TOE Interfaces

The requirements for the Functional Specifications for EAL4 are incremental to the requirements at EAL2. EAL2 requires that the ADV_FSP.2 requirements are met. EAL4 meets ADV_FSP.4. The tables below summarize these requirements. The ADV_FSP.4 (EAL4) table highlights the incremental differences from EAL2 in **bold-faced type**.

Note that the term TSF is used extensively by the CC standard to somehow differentiate the individual security functions within the TOE as opposed to the entire TOE. For most practical purposes, the terms TSF and TOE may be interchangeable in this book.

Also note that the term SFR-enforcing means that the interface plays a direct (as opposed to supporting) role in meeting the requirements in the Security Functional Requirement (SFR).

ADV_FSP.2 Security-enforcing functional specification

DEVELOPER ACTION ELEMENT	DESCRIPTION
ADV_FSP.2.1D	The developer shall provide a functional specification.
ADV_FSP.2.2D	The developer shall provide a tracing from the functional specification to the SFRs.
CONTENT AND PRESENTATION ELEMENTS	**DESCRIPTION**
ADV_FSP.2.1C	The functional specification shall completely represent the TSF.
ADV_FSP.2.2C	The functional specification shall describe the purpose and method of use for all TSFI.
ADV_FSP.2.3C	The functional specification shall identify and describe all parameters associated with each TSFI.
ADV_FSP.2.4C	For each SFR-enforcing TSFI, the functional specification shall describe the SFR-enforcing actions associated with the TSFI.
ADV_FSP.2.5C	For each SFR-enforcing TSFI, the functional specification shall describe direct error messages resulting from processing associated with the SFR-enforcing actions.
ADV_FSP.2.6C	The tracing shall demonstrate that the SFRs trace to TSFIs in the functional specification.

Table 38 - ADV_FSP.2 Requirements

ADV_FSP.4 Complete functional specification

DEVELOPER ACTION ELEMENT	DESCRIPTION
ADV_FSP.4.1D	The developer shall provide a functional specification.
ADV_FSP.4.2D	The developer shall provide a tracing from the functional specification to the SFRs.
CONTENT AND PRESENTATION ELEMENTS	**DESCRIPTION**
ADV_FSP.4.1C	The functional specification shall completely represent the TSF.

ADV_FSP.4.2C	The functional specification shall describe the purpose and method of use for all TSFI.
ADV_FSP.4.3C	The functional specification shall identify and describe all parameters associated with each TSFI.
ADV_FSP.4.4C	For each SFR-enforcing TSFI, the functional specification shall **describe all** actions associated with the TSFI.
ADV_FSP.4.5C	**The functional specification shall describe all direct error messages that may result from an invocation of each TSFI.**
ADV_FSP.4.6C	The tracing shall demonstrate that the SFRs trace to TSFIs in the functional specification.

Table 39 - ADV_FSP.4 Requirements

For TOEs that include hardware, physical interfaces shall be described including light-emitting diode (LED) indicator lights, network interface ports, and other physical connectors. How these physical connectors are used in the performance of the security functions shall be described. Illustrations similar to the example below can help the evaluator understand what the TOE physically looks like.

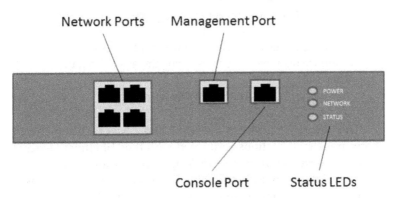

Figure 14 - Physical Interfaces

The contents of the TSFI descriptions are summarized in the table below.

Interface Name
Identifier for the TSFI
Purpose
Describes the purpose of the interface.
Method of Use
Describes the method of use of the interface and/or reference documentation containing the method of use.
Relevant SFRs
Lists the Security Functional Requirements supported by this interface.
Parameters
Lists the parameters used by the interface and/or reference documentation listing the parameters used by the interface.
Parameter Descriptions
Describes the parameters used by the interface and/or reference documentation describing the parameters used by the interface.
Actions
Describes the actions taken by the interface and/or reference documentation describing the actions taken by the interface.
Errors
Describes the error messages from the interface and/or reference documentation describing the errors from the interface.

Figure 15 - TSFI Description

The difference between the EAL2 and EAL4 requirements is that EAL4 requires that all actions associated with the TSFI must be described and all error messages from the TSFI must be documented. EAL2 just requires descriptions for SFR-enforcing actions and error messages.

It is often easier to reference user/administrator manuals (by chapter, section, and page number) to provide the details for how a user interface (UI) works. These manuals usually describe the purpose, have instructions on how to invoke the actions (i.e., method of use), and describe the input parameters.

Perhaps the area that causes commercial developers the most problems in developing the FSP is completing the error messages portion of the TSFI descriptions. What is often not readily available is a com-

140

plete list of error messages with good descriptions. For many application software TOEs, I have had to login to a test system and generate errors manually from the user interface to create this list. The other issue is aligning the error messages with the SFR-enforcing actions. Even at EAL2, the evaluator is instructed to "examine" (i.e., look closely at) the TSFI description to make sure they include error messages associated with SFR-enforcing actions. This makes the exercise of collecting the list of error messages more difficult as they should be only those associated with the SFRs – not just a dump of all error messages. Error message descriptions can also be tricky as some may be cryptic in their raw forms.

External interfaces to middleware, databases, operating systems, and other software can be described by referencing the vendor's application programmatic interface (API) documentation. Because these types of products expect other products to interface with them, there is ample documentation on the purpose, method of use, parameters, parameter descriptions, and errors. If a constrained set of APIs are used by the TOE, the evaluator may ask that the list of TOE-relevant APIs and errors be highlighted.

For network interfaces using standard protocols, the protocol standards (e.g., RFC) may be referenced. Again, if only certain protocol options are used by the TOE, the evaluator may ask that only the TOE-relevant information be provided so that they do not have to sort through the entire protocol standard to determine which actions and errors correspond to the SFRs.

Ensure completeness by checking to make sure that the interface descriptions cover all aspects of all of the SFRs. For example, FAU_GEN.1 requires that the TOE generate an audit log event for the start-up and shutdown of the audit functions. If the administrator interface provides a command to shut down the audit function, the administrator UI TSFI description should include the command used, parameter descriptions, and errors associated with that command. FAU_GEN.1 also requires that security events get logged (e.g., changes to the TOE configuration). This functionality shall also be described. The following example illustrates one way of presenting this information. Note that the References point to the Administrator's guide (ADMIN) which provides more details about the use of the commands.

TSFI	DESCRIPTION	RELEVANT SFRs	REFERENCE
Console > Admin > Shutdown	Console command to shut down the server. Click on the Shutdown button to stop the server audit functions.	FAU_GEN.1	(ADMIN) pg. 234
Console > Admin > Settings	Console command to configure the TOE. Click on Settings tab to show the configuration panel.	FAU_GEN.1 FMT_MTD.1	(ADMIN) pgs. 422-433

Figure 16 - Sample TSFI

The TSFI "sub-interfaces" in the example are identified with ">." Sub-interfaces are provided merely as a convenience to direct the evaluator to the right part of the interface and to the specific way in which the SFRs are satisfied. Technically, the TSFI in the example is Console.

Another example using a different format describes a network interface that conforms to a standard RFC specification is shown below.

RFC 894: IP Over Ethernet
Purpose:
Transmission of IP Datagrams over Ethernet Networks. See also RFC 791, Internet Protocol (http://tools.ietf.org/html/rfc894)
Method of Use:
See RFC 894. (http://tools.ietf.org/html/rfc894)
Relevant SFRs:
FAU_GEN.1 FDP_IFC.1 FDP_IFF.1
Parameters:
Frame type. See RFC 894, Frame Format Section and RFC 791, Section 3.1 Internet Header Format. The security relevant parameters are: • Protocol   • Source address   • Destination address   • Don't Fragment (DF) flag   • More Fragments (MF) flag   • Fragment Offset

RFC 894: IP Over Ethernet
Parameter Descriptions:
See RFC 894, Frame Format Section and RFC 791, Section 3.1
Actions:
The TOE filters protocol, source address, and destination address according to the security rules configured by the administrator. If the security rule is defined to log the action, the event is logged. The TOE applies the fragmentation and stateful packet inspection rules using information from this interface. The TOE also determines loopback and broadcast identifiers based on information from this interface. Source and destination zones and users are determined by IP addresses.
Errors:
Packets dropped: flow state receive error
Session setup: no destination zone from forwarding
Packets dropped: non-SYN TCP without session match
Packets dropped: IP TTL reaches zero
Packets dropped: Invalid IP version
Packets dropped: Packet too short to cover IP header
Packets dropped: IP packet truncated
Packets dropped: Zero TTL in IP packer
Packets dropped: TCP (UDP) packet too short
Packets dropped: TCP/UDP checksum failure

A handy illustration to include in the FSP is the TSFI-to-SFR mapping table. This table illustrates which SFRs are satisfied by which TSFI. The following table is an example. The "X" indicates that the TSFI enforces the SFR (SFR-enforcing) and the "S" indicates that the TSFI supports the SFR (SFR-supporting). Illustrating the SFR-supporting interfaces is provided only for completeness and is not a requirement at EAL2 or EAL4. Curiously, defining the SFR-supporting interfaces is a requirement for EAL3.

143

TSF	SFR	INTERFACE		
		CONSOLE	NETWORK	DB
Security Audit	FAU_GEN.1	X	X	
	FAU_SAR.1	X	X	
	FAU_STG.1			X
User Data	FDP_IFC.1		X	S
Protection	FDP_IFF.1		X	S
Identification	FIA_AFL.1	X		
and Authenti-	FIA_UAU.1	X	X	
cation	FIA_UID.2	X		
	FIA_USB.1	X		
Security	FMT_MOF.1	X		S
Management	FMT_MSA.1	X		
	FMT_MSA.3	X		
	FMT_MTD.1	X		S
	FMT_SMF.1	X	X	
	FMT_SMR.1	X		
Trusted	FTP_ITC.1		X	
Path/Channels	FTP_TRP.1	X	X	

Figure 17 - TSFI to SFR Mapping

Chapter 16: Basic Design (EAL2)

The TOE Design (TDS) documents for EAL2 and EAL4 are quite different. The TDS for EAL4 is a superset of the requirements for EAL2 and are described in Chapter 17: Modular Design (EAL4). This chapter deals with the EAL2 requirements for TDS.

The TDS for EAL2 (called Basic Design) describes the TOE in terms of subsystems. Subsystems are high-level components of the TOE that contribute (either enforce or support) toward meeting the Security Functional Requirements (SFRs) claimed in the Security Target (ST). The TDS also links the subsystems to the TOE Security Functional Interfaces (TSFI) that are defined in the Functional Specifications (FSP).

The requirements for the TDS for EAL2 are summarized in the table shown below.

ADV_TDS.1 Basic design

DEVELOPER ACTION ELEMENT	DESCRIPTION
ADV_TDS.1.1D	The developer shall provide the design of the TOE.
ADV_TDS.1.2D	The developer shall provide a mapping from the TSFI of the functional specification to the lowest level of decomposition available in the TOE design.
CONTENT AND PRESENTATION ELEMENTS	DESCRIPTION
ADV_TDS.1.1C	The design shall describe the structure of the TOE in terms of subsystems.
ADV_TDS.1.2C	The design shall identify all subsystems of the TSF.
ADV_TDS.1.3C	The design shall describe the behaviour of each SFR-supporting or SFR non-interfering TSF subsystem in sufficient detail to determine that it is not SFR-enforcing.
ADV_TDS.1.4C	The design shall summarise the SFR-enforcing behaviour of the SFR-enforcing subsystems.

ADV_TDS.1.5C	The design shall provide a description of the interactions among SFR-enforcing subsystems of the TSF, and between the SFR-enforcing subsystems of the TSF and other subsystems of the TSF.
ADV_TDS.1.6C	The mapping shall demonstrate that all TSFIs trace to the behaviour described in the TOE design that they invoke.

Table 40 - ADV_TDS.1 Requirements

The terms SFR-enforcing, SFR-supporting and SFR-non-interfering are used to describe the requirements for the TDS. The [CEM] provides the following definitions of these terms.

An SFR-supporting subsystem is one that is depended on by an SFR-enforcing subsystem in order to implement an SFR, but does not play as direct a role as an SFR-enforcing subsystem. An SFR-non-interfering subsystem is one that is not depended upon, in either a supporting or enforcing role, to implement an SFR.

My opinion is that the decomposition of the TOE should result in only subsystems that are SFR-enforcing or SFR-supporting. Otherwise, why are they part of the TOE which by definition provides the security functionality claimed in the ST?

While one could decompose a product into "physical" subsystems as defined by the developer, I have found that a TDS that decomposes the TOE into its "logical" security subsystems is easier to explain to the evaluator. It also avoids the aforementioned SFR-non-interfering subsystems.

An example of a physical decomposition is; a developer may describe their product in terms of an Administrator Console Subsystem, Server Subsystem and a Client Subsystem. The Console may act as the user interface for the administrator, the Server may contain all of the configuration functionality, and the Client Subsystem may be responsible for all of the operator user functions. This arrangement makes it more difficult to illustrate how the individual Security Functional Requirements (SFRs) are satisfied.

I have found that using the "logical" decomposition of the TOE into subsystems such as Audit Subsystem, Management Subsystem, Policy Enforcement Subsystem, and Communications Subsystem are more easily mapped to the SFRs as shown in the following example. The

146

logical Policy Enforcement Subsystem may actually be implemented in both the physical Server and the Client subsystems.

SUBSYSTEM	RELEVANT SFRs
Audit Subsystem	FAU_GEN.1 (supporting) FAU_SAR.1 (enforcing) FAU_STG.1 (enforcing)
Management Subsystem	FAU_GEN.1 (enforcing) FMT_MOF.1 (enforcing) FMT_MTD.1 (enforcing) FMT_MSA.1 (enforcing) FMT_MSA.3 (enforcing) FMT_SMF.1 (enforcing) FMT_SMR.1 (enforcing)
Policy Enforcement Subsystem	FDP_ACC.1 (enforcing) FDP_ACF.1 (enforcing) FDP_IFC.1 (enforcing) FDP_IFF.1 (enforcing)
Communications Subsystem	FAU_GEN.1 (enforcing) FCS_CKM.1 (enforcing) FCS_CKM.4 (enforcing) FCS_COP.1 (enforcing) FPT_ITT.1 (enforcing) FTP_ITC.1 (enforcing) FTP_TRP.1 (enforcing)

Table 41 - Example Subsystems

The example table also points out the role each subsystem plays toward meeting the SFRs. Note that the Audit Subsystem "supports" the FAU_GEN.1 SFR. This means that the Audit Subsystem itself does not generate auditable events but does play a supporting role for other subsystems to record the audit event. This table can serve to address the ADV_TDS.1.1C - 3C content requirements.

Diagrams are very helpful to the evaluator to visualize the connections between subsystems and external interfaces. The following figure is an example of such a diagram.

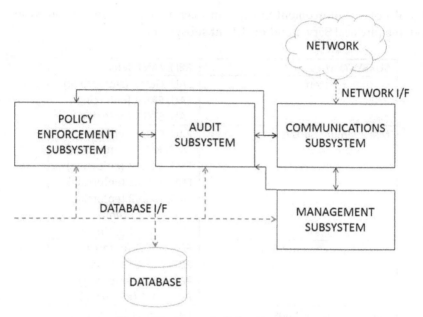

Figure 18 - Example Subsystem Diagram

This diagram illustrates the connections and interactions between the different TOE subsystems as well as the relevant external interfaces (TSFI) associated with the subsystems. This diagram shall support and be consistent with the subsystem descriptions provided in the TDS.

Subsystem Description Creation Tip

I have found that a handy way to ensure that all of the SFRs are covered in the TDS and that the subsystem descriptions are complete is to first trace all of the security functions through the subsystems responsible for the functionality. This "functional thread" as I call it can be collected with other threads that pass through a subsystem to produce the subsystem description. For example, the following diagram shows a subset of the subsystems from the example shown earlier in this chapter. This diagram will be used to illustrate how the example TOE's subsystems implement the Security Management (FMT) and Security Audit (FAU) security functions.

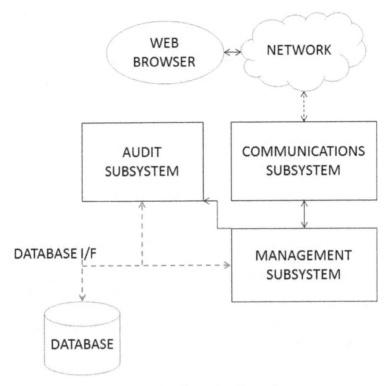

Figure 19 - Configuration Example

Here is the example of a "functional thread" illustrated by the figure above. From the web browser, an already-authenticated user accesses the TOE's configuration screens.

1. The web browser uses the Network Interface TSFI to connect to the Communications Subsystem.
2. The Communications Subsystem requests the current configuration settings from the Management Subsystem.
3. The Management Subsystem requests and receives the database records from the database via the Database TSFI.
4. The Management Subsystem forwards the current settings back to the Communications Subsystem.
5. The current configuration values are sent back to the user via the Network TSFI.

6. The changes to the configuration parameter values that the user makes are passed via the Network TSFI to the Communications Subsystem.
7. The Communications Subsystem sends the changes to the Management Subsystem.
8. The Management Subsystem sends the modifications to the database via the Database Interface TSFI.
9. In addition, the Management Subsystem sends the modification information (along with user identification and date/time stamps) to the Audit Subsystem.
10. The Audit Subsystem logs the configuration modification event to the database also using the Database TSFI.

This sequence illustrates how the TOE subsystems enforce and support FMT_MTD.1 (Management of TSF data) and FAU_GEN.1 (Audit data generation).

To complete the TDS, this exercise is repeated for each function that demonstrates the claimed SFRs until the complete implementation of each SFR has been covered. Subsystem descriptions can be developed using the information from their contributions (i.e., SFR-enforcing or SFR-supporting) in these "functional threads."

Subsystem Descriptions

Perhaps the most convenient way to format the TDS is to provide a section for each subsystem. Each section should cover the following topics intended to address ADV_TDS.1.4C – 6C:

- Purpose – general statements about the functionality provided by the subsystem.
- Security Functionality – specific statements about which SFRs are addressed by the subsystem and how (i.e., what SFR-relevant actions does the subsystem perform). It should be made apparent whether the subsystem actions are SFR-enforcing or SFR-supporting.
- Internal Interfaces and Interactions – descriptions of the connections to other subsystems including descriptions of the data and control information exchanged during the performance of the security functions. The interactions description will describe the actions taken by the subsystem.

150

- External Interfaces – descriptions of the TSFI connected to the subsystem. It describes what data is exchanged and what actions the subsystem takes.

The following is an example of the description of a subsystem that is both SFR-enforcing and SFR-supporting.

Audit Subsystem

Purpose:
The Audit Subsystem collects security events generated from other TOE subsystems and stores the records. This subsystem also provides a means to review audit records to authorized users.

Security Functionality:

SFR	FUNCTIONALITY
FAU_GEN.1 (supporting)	This subsystem supports the FAU_GEN.1.2 by recording the audit records generated by other TOE subsystems.
FAU_SAR.1 (enforcing)	This subsystem enforces FAU_SAR.1 by providing authorized users a means to review audit records. It reads the audit records from the audit log storage and presents the records in a readable fashion to the users.
FAU_STG.1 (enforcing)	This subsystem enforces FAU_STG.1 by preventing the deletion of stored audit records. This subsystem prevents the deletion of audit records by not providing any means to delete records.

Internal Interfaces and Interactions:

INTERNAL INTERFACE	DESCRIPTION AND INTERACTIONS
Audit → Communications	The Communications subsystem sends communication channel initiation, termination, and failure event data to the Audit subsystem for recording in the audit logs. The Audit subsystem sends audit log records to the Communications subsystem to present to authorized users for review.
Audit → Management	The Management subsystem sends configuration and policy modification data to the Audit subsystem for recording in the audit logs.
Audit → Policy Enforcement	The Policy Enforcement subsystem sends policy violation data to the Audit subsystem for recording in the audit logs.

External Interfaces:

TSFI INTERFACE	DESCRIPTION
Audit → Database	The Audit subsystem sends audit log records to the Database for storage. The Audit subsystem retrieves audit log records for presentation and review to the authorized users.

Subsystems are considered to be SFR-enforcing when that subsystem directly provides the functionality that implements an SFR. In the above example, the Audit subsystem enforces FAU_SAR.1 as defined in [CC2].

FAU_SAR.1 Audit review

FAU_SAR.1.1   The TSF shall provide [assignment: authorised users] with the capability to read [assignment: list of audit information] from the audit records.

FAU_SAR.1.2 The TSF shall provide the audit records in a manner suitable for the user to interpret the information.

The Audit subsystem enforces FAU_SAR.1 by providing the audit records in a "suitable manner" only to authorized users thus satisfying FAU_SAR.1.1 and 1.2.

The high-level descriptions do not need to include specific data structures but covers more general data flow, message flow, and control relationships within a subsystem. The goal of these descriptions is to give the evaluator enough information to understand how the SFR-enforcing behavior is achieved. That means providing descriptions that cover all of the specific requirements within each SFR.

Consistency between subsystem descriptions is important in the TDS. To that end, the other subsystem descriptions must mirror the descriptions of the internal interfaces to one another. In the example above, the Communications subsystem description should include the internal interface description shown below to match the Audit → Communications internal interface described in the Audit subsystem description.

INTERNAL INTERFACE	DESCRIPTION AND INTERACTIONS
Communications → Audit	The Communications subsystem receives audit log records from the Audit subsystem to present to authorized users for review. The Communications subsystem sends communication channel initiation, termination, and failure event data to the Audit subsystem for recording in the audit logs.

The set of external interfaces must be consistent with the TSFI described in the Functional Specifications (FSP) document. A table summarizing the coverage of the TSFI is useful to the evaluator to check that the coverage is complete as shown in this example. The "X" indicates that the subsystem has a direct connection to the TSFI. This summary table must be consistent with the subsystem descriptions and with any diagrams used in the TDS and FSP.

TSFI	SUBSYSTEM			
	AUDIT	MGMT	COMMS	POLICY
DATABASE	X	X		X
NETWORK			X	

Another handy table to include in the TDS is a mapping table between the subsystems and SFRs. This table is provided as a convenience to the evaluator and the trick is to make sure it is consistent with the descriptions of the subsystems. In the example below, "E" indicates that the subsystem enforces the SFR. "S" indicates that the subsystem supports the SFR.

SFR	SUBSYSTEM			
	AUDIT	MGMT	COMMS	POLICY
FAU_GEN.1	S	E	E	E
FAU_SAR.1	E		S	
FAU_STG.1	E			
FDP_IFC.1				E
FDP_IFF.1				E
FMT_MOF.1		E		
FMT_MSA.1		E		
FMT_MSA.3		E		
FMT_MTD.1		E		
FMT_SMF.1		E		
FMT_SMR.1		E		
FTP_ITC.1			E	
FTP_TRP.1			E	

Chapter 17: Modular Design (EAL4)

The TOE Design (TDS) document for EAL4 called the Modular Design is perhaps the most arduous document to put together. This document requires deep technical understanding of the TOE internal design and implementation. It also requires discipline to map the proper design and implementation information to the TDS.

My objectives for this chapter are to provide information and insights that:

- Make it easier for developers to create the Modular Design document.
- Make it easier for the evaluators to complete their evaluation of the Modular Design document.

Where the TDS for EAL2 (Basic Design) decomposes the TOE into high-level subsystems, the TDS for EAL4 (Modular Design) describes the TOE in terms of lower-level modules. A key distinction between subsystems and modules is that subsystems are logical components of security functions whereas modules are reflections of the physical components of the TOE. A subsystem decomposition is a description of the TOE to provide a high-level description of what a portion of the TOE is doing and how. A module is a detailed description of the TOE implementation.

For software TOEs, modules may be processes, or libraries. For hardware, modules may be printed circuit boards (PCBs), integrated circuits (ICs), or blades.

The requirements for the TDS for EAL4 are summarized in the following table.

ADV_TDS.3 Modular design

DEVELOPER ACTION ELEMENT	DESCRIPTION
ADV_TDS.3.1D	The developer shall provide the design of the TOE.
ADV_TDS.3.2D	The developer shall provide a mapping from the TSFI of the functional specification to the lowest level of decomposition available in the TOE design.

CONTENT AND PRESENTATION ELEMENTS	DESCRIPTION
ADV_TDS.3.1C	The design shall describe the structure of the TOE in terms of subsystems.
ADV_TDS.3.2C	The design shall describe the TSF in terms of modules.
ADV_TDS.3.3C	The design shall identify all subsystems of the TSF.
ADV_TDS.3.4C	The design shall provide a description of each subsystem of the TSF.
ADV_TDS.3.5C	The design shall provide a description of the interactions among all subsystems of the TSF.
ADV_TDS.3.6C	The design shall provide a mapping from the subsystems of the TSF to the modules of the TSF.
ADV_TDS.3.7C	The design shall describe each SFR-enforcing module in terms of its purpose and relationship with other modules.
ADV_TDS.3.8C	The design shall describe each SFR-enforcing module in terms of its SFR-related interfaces, return values from those interfaces, interaction with other modules and called SFR-related interfaces to other SFR-enforcing modules.
ADV_TDS.3.9C	The design shall describe each SFR-supporting or SFR-non-interfering module in terms of its purpose and interaction with other modules.
ADV_TDS.3.10C	The mapping shall demonstrate that all TSFIs trace to the behaviour described in the TOE design that they invoke.

Table 42 - ADV_TDS.3 Requirements

The Modular Design requirements are a superset of the EAL2 Basic Design requirements (see Chapter 16: Basic Design (EAL2) for more details on the Basic Design). In addition to describing the TOE in terms of logical subsystems (as with EAL2), the Modular Design document must also describe the TOE in terms of modules (within those subsystems). EAL4 includes the ADV_IMP.1: Implementation representation of the TSF (see also Chapter 18: Implementation Representation (EAL4)) which includes the following requirement and a dependency on ADV_TDS.3.

ADV_IMP.1.2D   The developer shall provide a mapping between the TOE design description and the sample of the implementation representation.

The modules included in the Modular Design document must be mapped to the implementation representation. For software TOEs, this means the module source code, application programmatic interfaces (APIs), header files, and function calls may be examined by the evaluators to verify the Modular Design descriptions.

The description of ADV_TDS in the CC standards [CC3] includes the statement "A developer should be able to implement the part of the TOE described by the module with no further design decisions." This is ludicrous but I've had evaluators quote this to me when they felt there was not enough detail given about how the module performs their portions of the security functions. Details such as what decisions the module makes based on what inputs and criteria should be provided. The details of any algorithms used by the module may not have to be provided but the fact that the module uses an algorithm does; as well as what actions the module performs based on the output of that algorithm.

Diagrams depicting the subsystems and modules within the TOE help the evaluator understand the structure, interfaces, and interactions of the TOE. The following is an example of a diagram illustrating the TOE subsystems, modules, and interfaces.

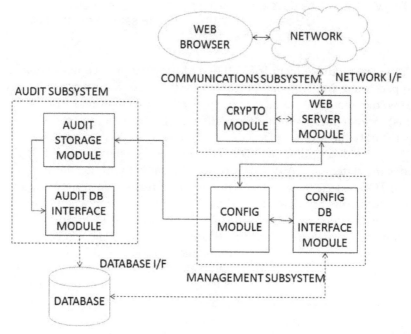

Figure 20 - Example TOE Subsystems and Modules

The Modular Design document can be organized by subsystem. Below is a partial outline for the Modular Design document describing the TOE illustrated in the figure above.

Audit Subsystem
1. Audit Subsystem Purpose
2. Audit Subsystem Security Functionality
3. Audit Subsystem Interactions
4. Audit Subsystem Interfaces
5. Audit Subsystem Modules
   a. Audit Storage Module
      i. Audit Storage Module Purpose
      ii. Audit Storage Module Security Functionality
      iii. Audit Storage Module Interfaces
      iv. Audit Storage Module Interactions
         1. Configuration Management
         2. User Policy Management
         3. ...
   b. Audit DB Interface Module
      i. Audit DB Interface Module Purpose

158

ii. Audit DB Interface Module Security Functionality
iii. Audit DB Interface Module Interfaces
iv. Audit DB Interface Module Interactions
1. Configuration Management
2. User Policy Management
3. ...

Communications Subsystem

...

The Subsystem Purpose, Security Functionality, Interactions, and Interfaces are identical to the content used to meet the EAL2 requirements. See Chapter 16: Basic Design (EAL2) - Subsystem Descriptions for more details. The ADV_TDS.3.2C adds the requirement to describe the TOE in terms of modules.

The following diagram illustrates an example Audit Subsystem with its constituent modules and interfaces. This type of diagram satisfies the ADV_TDS.3.6C requirement and helps to reinforce the textual descriptions about the subsystem and its modules.

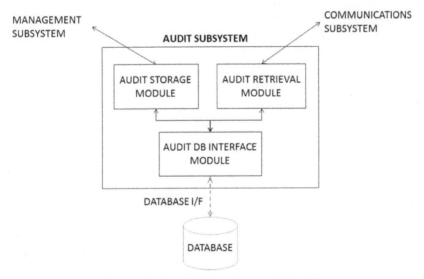

Figure 21 - Audit Subsystem and Modules

Module Description Creation Tip

In Chapter 16: Basic Design (EAL2) - Subsystem Description Creation Tip, I shared a technique I use to create the subsystem descriptions in the TDS for EAL2. This technique becomes even more useful for developing module descriptions for the Modular Design document. There are far more modules to describe than subsystems and more detail needs to be provided for module descriptions than subsystems. My technique helps keep things organized and reduces the chance that something will get overlooked.

Another handy technique is to subdivide the Security Functionality descriptions by "functional thread" (e.g., Configuration changes or user policy management). This will help the evaluator determine how each aspect of each SFR is covered by the subsystems and can help the evaluator understand how the product features map to each of the SFRs (which will be important during the Testing phase).

At the module level, tracing through a "functional thread" is a form of a high-level code walk-through. Traditional code walk-throughs are very detailed because they are intended to mimic the computer's execution of the code. The "functional thread" exercise is done at a higher-level and is intended to follow the code execution path through the key modules. See Appendix A: Modular Design Example for an illustration of using the "functional thread" exercise to generate a module description.

Tracing through the execution path of each SFR-enforcing and SFR-supporting module for each SFR requires that the modular decomposition of the TOE lends itself to do this tracing. In my discussions with developers, what constitutes a module for these purposes takes some thought. Commercial software may not be implemented in ways that make it easy to define where a module boundary (for CC purposes) is.

Sometimes a module can conveniently be defined as a process (e.g., a Microsoft Windows-based application or service with the .exe suffix) or a library (with the .lib suffix). Other times a module may be a code function (or in object-oriented code, a method or object). The trick is to define the module such that the evaluator can easily find the corresponding source code during the Implementation Representation evaluation and that the interfaces and interactions can be clearly described.

Module Descriptions

Unlike subsystems, modules describe the implementation in a level of detail that can serve as a guide to reviewing the implementation representation (e.g., source code). According to the [CEM], the description should be such that one could create an implementation of the module from the description. The evaluators need enough detail to understand how the module interacts with other modules, how it uses the interfaces (e.g., TSFI), and what actions it takes based on the inputs it receives. The descriptions must fully explain how the module is SFR-enforcing and across all of the module descriptions, it must be clear as to how all of the SFR requirements are met. These descriptions will be verified during the Implementation Representation evaluation.

The TDS for EAL2 (Basic Design) describes the internal interfaces and interactions between subsystems. This is a relatively simple exercise because the descriptions do not have to be very detailed and there are usually only a few subsystems. For EAL4, the interaction descriptions must be much more detailed and there can be a lot more modules.

The different module description sub-sections are described in the following sections and an example is provided in Appendix A: Modular Design Example.

Module Purpose

The Module Purpose describes how the module contributes (e.g., SFR-enforcing and SFR-supporting) to all of the affected security functions. This should summarize all of the actions the module takes that enforce or support the SFRs and serves as a lead-in to the Module Security Functionality section.

Module Security Functionality

The Module Security Functionality section provides the linkages between the SFRs and the module functionality. The functionality description should provide the evidence to support the claims that the module enforces or supports the individual SFRs. This information can be provided in a table such as the following example.

161

SFR	FUNCTIONALITY
FAU_GEN.1 (enforcing)	The Module generates an audit event when the user attempts to login to the TOE console. The Module includes in the audit event record the date and time of the event, the user name, the event type (login), and the success or failure of the login attempt.
FIA_UID.2 (enforcing)	The Module will check user identity before allowing the user to access TOE functions.
FIA_UAU.2 (enforcing)	The Module will check user authentication credentials before allowing the user to access TOE functions.

Module Interfaces

The Module Interfaces section describes the interfaces the module exposes to other modules. This amounts to the application programmatic interface (API) descriptions for each function provided by the module. Below is an example. Note that not every API provided by the module needs to be described, just those that used to enforce or support the SFRs.

INTERFACE	
API	
`write_data(handle_t *h, char module_data_name, char *data, int error_status))`	
PURPOSE	
Writes the input data buffer to the logs recording the module ID that generated the entry.	
PARAMETER	**PARAMETER DESCRIPTION**
*h	Context information
module_data_name	Originating module name
*data	Log data
RETURN VALUES	
error_status = 0 for success; -1 for failure	

Module Interactions

The Module Interactions section describes the module's role for each applicable "functional thread." This produces the complete set of

162

module interactions. These descriptions are intended to explain to the evaluator how the module supports or enforces the claimed SFRs.

It is handy to provide a summary of interactions for the module. That summary can be provided in a table such as the one below. It describes the interfaces used by the module, what module provides the interface, and the purpose of the interface. These interfaces and interactions shall be described in further detail in the Module Interactions section.

SUBSYSTEM - MODULE	INTERFACE	ACTION
Communications Subsystem – Web Server Module	receive_config_command	Receive commands from the Web Server.
	send_old_config_to_user	Send current configuration settings to the Web Server module.
Management Subsystem – Config DB Interface Module	write_new_DB_record	Sends the new configuration settings to the database.
Audit Subsystem – Audit Storage Module	send_audit_event	Sends audit event to audit log.

Subdividing the Module Interactions section into use cases based on the "functional threads" makes it easier to link the TOE security functions to the module actions and interactions. For example, the Configuration Module may handle the management of the TOE configurations and user policies. Each of these "use cases" can be described in separate sub-sections of the Module Interactions section as illustrated in the following.

Configuration Module Description

Module Interactions

Use Case 1: TOE Configuration
The Configuration Module receives configuration changes through the API provided by the Console Module.

INTERFACE	
PROVIDER	
Communications Subsystem – Console Module	
API	
`receive_config_command (cfg_buffer)`	
PURPOSE	
Receive configuration command from the web server module. This command originated from the user.	
PARAMETER	**PARAMETER DESCRIPTION**
cfg_buffer	Configuration buffer
RETURN VALUES	
N/A	

The Configuration Module sends the configuration information to the database using the following API....

Use Case 2: User Policy Management
The Configuration Module receives user policy update data from the Admin Module.

INTERFACE	
PROVIDER	
Administrator Subsystem – Admin Module	
API	
`receive_admin_command (admin_buffer)`	
PURPOSE	
Receive administrator commands from the Admin module. This command originated from the local administrator.	
PARAMETER	**PARAMETER DESCRIPTION**
admin_buffer	Configuration buffer
RETURN VALUES	
N/A	

The Configuration Module parses the admin_buffer and checks the validity of the commands using the following API.

INTERFACE	
PROVIDER	
Administrator Subsystem – Verification Module	
API	
`verify_admin_command (admin_buffer)`	

INTERFACE	
PURPOSE	
Verifies administrator commands.	
PARAMETER	**PARAMETER DESCRIPTION**
admin_buffer	Configuration buffer
RETURN VALUES	
0 = success; -1 = failure	

Note that the interfaces may be TOE Security Functional Interfaces (TSFI) to external entities. The Modular Design document must cover all of the TSFI described in the Functional Specifications document (FSP). These descriptions are intended to address the ADV_TDS.3.10C requirement. These interfaces may be described in the following form.

TSF INTERFACE	
TSFI	
Database Interface	
API	
`SELECT column_list FROM table-name`	
`[WHERE Clause]`	
`[GROUP BY clause]`	
`[HAVING clause]`	
`[ORDER BY clause]`	
PURPOSE	
SQL SELECT statement is used to query or retrieve data from a table in the database.	
PARAMETER	**PARAMETER DESCRIPTION**
column_list	Columns = "Config parms"
table-name	TOE_Configuration
WHERE Clause	Where "date" < TODAY
GROUP BY clause	Group by "zone"
HAVING clause	Having "IP" = 192.92.1.1
ORDER BY clause	Order by "ID"
RETURN VALUES	
Database records	

Chapter 18: Implementation Representation (EAL4)

The Implementation Representation is required at EAL4. The Implementation Representation may be software source code, firmware source code, hardware diagrams and/or IC hardware design language code or layout data. The Implementation Representation is used to demonstrate that the TOE conforms to its design (TDS) and to provide a basis for the search for vulnerabilities (AVA_VAN).

A key way in which evaluators will analyze the Modular Design document is to examine a sample of the module interfaces. The Application Programmatic Interfaces (APIs) described in the Modular Design document must be reflected in the Implementation Representation. Evaluators will also verify that the SFR-enforcing and SFR-supporting actions described in the Modular Design document are reflected in the Implementation Representation.

The following are the requirements for the Implementation Representation. Generally, there is no additional documentation produced to satisfy these requirements. The developer need only make available the source code or hardware design language code to the evaluator to assess against the design document. All of the documentation effort is in creating the Modular Design document.

ADV_IMP.1 Implementation representation of the TSF

DEVELOPER ACTION ELEMENT	DESCRIPTION
ADV_IMP.1.1D	The developer shall make available the implementation representation for the entire TSF.
ADV_IMP.1.2D	The developer shall provide a mapping between the TOE design description and the sample of the implementation representation.
CONTENT AND PRESENTATION ELEMENTS	DESCRIPTION
ADV_IMP.1.1C	The implementation representation shall define the TSF to a level of detail such that the TSF can be generated without further design decisions.

ADV_IMP.1.2C	The implementation representation shall be in the form used by the development personnel.
ADV_IMP.1.3C	The mapping between the TOE design description and the sample of the implementation representation shall demonstrate their correspondence.

Table 43 - ADV_IMP.1 Requirements

Evaluators may request specific pieces of Implementation Representation for the sampling required in ADV_IMP.1.2D. They may not need any documentation to help them identify the relevant samples but the developer probably will be called upon to locate those specific pieces of source code. Their selection of the samples will depend on areas they would like to explore further to verify the implementation or may be areas of potential security weakness.

Developers generally guard their Implementation Representations very carefully and allowing a third-party to examine it usually requires executive approval. In most of the projects I've been involved in that required inspection of source code, the developer insisted that additional intellectual property (IP) protection agreements are in place with the evaluation lab. Moreover, developers want to ensure that they control access by allowing access to the source code only on their premises. This review may be added to the site visit along with the lifecycle processes verifications and any on-site product testing.

PART VI: GUIDANCE AND TESTING

This part contains:

Chapter 19: Operational and Preparative Guidance
Chapter 20: Test Plan
Chapter 21: Vulnerability Analysis

Chapter 19: Operational and Preparative Guidance

In most CC evaluations (EAL2 and EAL4), a separate guidance document needs to be produced to supplement the existing user documentation (e.g., user guide, administrator guide, and installation guide). This supplementary guide will reference the standard product documentation but will provide more specific directions to evaluators and customers on how to put the TOE into the "evaluated configuration" and how to operate the TOE "securely." This document is sometimes referred to as the Operational User Guidance and Preparative Procedures or Guidance document. Note that all user guides referenced by the Guidance document shall also be provided to the evaluators.

This supplementary document will need to be made available to the customers. Oftentimes, developers will make it available for download or upon request for those customers who want to use the TOE in the evaluated configuration. Evaluators will ask how this document will be made available to customers.

This document will also be used to guide the evaluator in preparing the TOE for testing. The evaluator will follow the steps a customer would take to take delivery of the TOE, install it, configure it, and operate it in order to demonstrate the claimed security functionality.

The Guidance document is intended to meet the following CC assurance requirements. A single document can meet the requirements for the two Guidance (AGD) areas:

- Preparative procedures
- Operational user guidance

AGD_PRE.1 Preparative procedures

DEVELOPER ACTION ELEMENT	DESCRIPTION
AGD_PRE.1.1D	The developer shall provide the TOE including its preparative procedures.
CONTENT AND PRESENTATION ELEMENTS	DESCRIPTION

171

AGD_PRE.1.1C	The preparative procedures shall describe all the steps necessary for secure acceptance of the delivered TOE in accordance with the developer's delivery procedures.
AGD_PRE.1.2C	The preparative procedures shall describe all the steps necessary for secure installation of the TOE and for the secure preparation of the operational environment in accordance with the security objectives for the operational environment as described in the ST.

Table 44 – AGD_PRE.1 Requirements

AGD_OPE.1 Operational user guidance

DEVELOPER ACTION ELEMENT	DESCRIPTION
AGD_OPE.1.1D	The developer shall provide operational user guidance.
CONTENT AND PRESENTATION ELEMENTS	DESCRIPTION
AGD_OPE.1.1C	The operational user guidance shall describe, for each user role, the user-accessible functions and privileges that should be controlled in a secure processing environment, including appropriate warnings.
AGD_OPE.1.2C	The operational user guidance shall describe, for each user role, how to use the available interfaces provided by the TOE in a secure manner.
AGD_OPE.1.3C	The operational user guidance shall describe, for each user role, the available functions and interfaces, in particular all security parameters under the control of the user, indicating secure values as appropriate.
AGD_OPE.1.4C	The operational user guidance shall, for each user role, clearly present each type of security-relevant event relative to the user-accessible functions that need to be performed, including changing the security characteristics of entities under the control of the TSF.

AGD_OPE.1.5C	The operational user guidance shall identify all possible modes of operation of the TOE (including operation following failure or operational error),
AGD_OPE.1.6C	The operational user guidance shall, for each user role, describe the security measures to be followed in order to fulfill the security objectives for the operational environment as described in the ST.
AGD_OPE.1.7C	The operational user guidance shall be clear and reasonable.

Table 45 – AGD_OPE.1 Requirements

Preparative Procedures

The Preparative Procedures section of the Guidance document describes from the customer's perspective how the TOE will be securely delivered, installed, and initially configured to meet the security requirements claimed in the Security Target (ST). This describes all of the steps a customer must follow prior to using the TOE.

There are 4 main topics covered by the Preparative Procedures section of the Guidance document.

- Preparing the Operational Environment
- Secure Delivery
- Installation
- Initial Configuration

Preparing the Operational Environment

This section of the Guidance document is intended to address the AGD_PRE.1.2C and AGD_OPE.1.6C requirements by ensuring that all of the assumptions and objectives for the Operational Environment as stated in the ST are met. This will include installing the TOE on the supported platforms and installing all of the prerequisite software (as defined in the TOE Description of the ST). The Preparative Procedures should describe how to meet all of the Assumptions described in the Security Problem Definition and all of the Objectives of the Operational Environment in the ST.

Many developers support their products on a wide range of platforms. These products include an installation guide to provide installation instructions specific to the particular platforms. For example, there

173

may be specific instructions for installing the product on a Linux operating system that are different from the instructions given for installing on a Windows operating system. Most commercial products support a range of platforms. In order to manage the scope of the CC evaluation, most commercial products will claim a smaller set of platforms in the evaluated configuration. The Guidance document will provide instructions to the customer directing them to install the TOE on only the platform(s) included in the evaluated configuration listed in the TOE Description of the ST.

Product installation guides also include instructions on installing any additional prerequisite software such as web servers, databases, and network time protocol (NTP) servers. The Guidance document will refer to these instructions but if there are any restrictions or particular configuration requirements of those components required to support the evaluated configuration of the TOE, the Preparative Procedures will provide those additional instructions. For example, the standard installation guide may provide instructions on how to install the required Apache web server but the Preparative Procedures should provide the specific instructions on how to configure the web server to only use Transport Layer Security (TLS) v1.2 algorithms in order to ensure that the cryptographic algorithms claimed in FCS_COP.1 are used by the TOE.

The Preparative Procedures must provide instructions to the customers on how to meet the Assumptions and Objectives of the Operational Environment defined in the ST. These assumptions often include assumptions about the physical deployment environment, personnel requirements, and other procedural/policy requirements that are outside of the scope of the TOE. For example, if the ST includes an Objective of the Operational Environment that the server portion of the TOE shall be deployed in a secure facility, the Preparative Procedures shall provide instructions to the customer that the server shall be installed in a secure facility. Also, if there is an objective that administrators shall install and use the TOE securely, the Preparative Procedures should instruct the customer to properly train the administrators on secure operational procedures.

Secure Delivery

Once the Operational Environment is prepared, the customer is ready for the secure delivery of the TOE. The Preparative Procedures section on secure delivery is intended to address the AGD_PRE.1.1C requirement. This information must be consistent (if not directly copied from) the Delivery (ALC_DEL.1) document. The Delivery document describes the end-to-end delivery process whereas the Preparative Procedures just deals with the customer end of the process. The Preparative Procedures presents instructions that the customer must follow for secure delivery and acceptance of the TOE.

Secure delivery and acceptance instructions to the customer may include checking shipping labels and serial numbers on hardware. Software download instructions should include steps that ensure that the correct version of the TOE is selected and that the download site can be verified. Instructions on checking the correct and complete delivery of the TOE should also be included such as software checksum or digital signature verification. These types of instructions can be copied from the Delivery document.

Installation

Commercial products generally have ample instructions to customers on how to install the product. As mentioned earlier any platform-specific instructions should be highlighted for platforms supported in the "evaluated configuration." Once installed, the customers should be given detailed instructions on how to verify that the installation completed correctly (including any self-test execution) and that the correct version of the TOE has been installed. The Preparative Procedures should also include instructions to the customer in the event that the installation fails.

Initial Configuration

After installation of the TOE is complete and verified, there may need to be some initial configurations to ensure that the Security Functional Requirements (SFRs) are met by the TOE. Some of these configurations may include:

- Configuring default user accounts or user roles
- Configuring default parameter settings
- Configuring cryptographic algorithms
- Disabling or advising customers not to use features that were outside the scope of the evaluation
- Enabling options to support TOE security features such as audit logging levels or secure communications

175

These configurations are all dependent upon what capabilities and options the product offers and what SFRs are claimed by the TOE. Generally, references to the standard product guides are used with the necessary options selected.

Operational User Guidance

The Operational User Guidance portion of the Guidance document is mostly a supplement to the product user guides. The combination of the product user guides and the Operational User Guidance should satisfy the AGD_OPE.1 requirements for content and presentation.

Requirements AGD_OPE.1.1C - AGD_OPE.1.4C have to do with user roles, their privileges and how users access their permitted functions. The Operational User Guidance may (if necessary) specify the user roles that are supported by the TOE (as defined in FMT_SMR.1). The rest of the required information is generally made available in the standard product guides. Any restrictions to the user roles required to fulfill the SFRs should be described in the Operational User Guidance along with instructions on how to set those restrictions.

It may be helpful to the evaluators to summarize the user roles and the permissions they are granted. This can come in the form of a table such as the one below.

USER ROLE	PERMISSIONS
Security Administrator	Configure secure communications Manage user accounts Manage mobile user security policies Review audit records
Device Administrator	Manage mobile device settings Review device audit records
Mobile User	Access mobile applications Manage mobile device settings

Requirement AGD_OPE.1.5C deals with describing the approved modes of operation. Product guides generally describe all modes of product operation but not all of these modes may be supported in the "evaluated configuration." Customers should be instructed to use only modes of operation that are supported by the TOE or given instructions on how to disable the non-supported modes.

176

While user guides generally provide a fairly complete description of product functionality, the evaluators are instructed to look for some particular pieces of information that may not always be included in customer product manuals such as the following.

- Security-related errors and failures and what actions users should take
- Default configuration setting values
- How to select more secure configuration setting values
- How to set secure password compositions
- Suggested frequency of user file backups

Chapter 20: Test Plan

The Test Plan is a combination of test setup instructions, test steps, and test results. Mappings to security functions (SFRs), interfaces (TSFIs), and subsystems/modules are required for EAL4. The Test Plan document shall cover the requirements for functional, depth, coverage, and independent testing. The requirements differ for EAL2 and EAL4 as summarized in the following tables.

EAL2 ATE Requirements

ASSURANCE CLASS	COMPONENTS
ATE: Tests	ATE_COV.1 Evidence of coverage
	ATE_FUN.1 Functional testing
	ATE_IND.2 Independent testing - sample

Table 46 - ATE Requirements for EAL2

ATE_COV.1 Evidence of coverage

DEVELOPER ACTION ELEMENT	DESCRIPTION
ATE_COV.1.1D	The developer shall provide evidence of the test coverage.
CONTENT AND PRESENTATION ELEMENTS	**DESCRIPTION**
ATE_COV.1.1C	The evidence of the test coverage shall show the correspondence between the tests in the test documentation and the TSFIs in the functional specification.

ATE_FUN.1 Functional testing

DEVELOPER ACTION ELEMENT	DESCRIPTION
ATE_FUN.1.1D	The developer shall test the TSF and document the results.

CONTENT AND PRESENTATION ELEMENTS	DESCRIPTION
ATE_FUN.1.2D	The developer shall provide test documentation.

ATE_IND.2 Independent testing - sample

DEVELOPER ACTION ELEMENT	DESCRIPTION
ATE_IND.2.1D	The developer shall provide the TOE for testing.
CONTENT AND PRESENTATION ELEMENTS	DESCRIPTION
ATE_IND.2.1C	The TOE shall be suitable for testing.
ATE_IND.2.2C	The developer shall provide an equivalent set of resources to those that were used in the developer's functional testing of the TSF.

EAL4 ATE Requirements

The incremental requirements over the EAL2 ATE requirements are highlighted in **bold** text in the tables below.

ASSURANCE CLASS	COMPONENTS
ATE: Tests	**ATE_COV.2 Analysis of coverage**
	ATE_DPT.1 Testing: basic design
	ATE_FUN.1 Functional testing
	ATE_IND.2 Independent testing - sample

Table 47 - ATE Requirements for EAL4

ATE_COV.2 Analysis of coverage

DEVELOPER ACTION ELEMENT	DESCRIPTION
ATE_COV.2.1D	The developer shall provide an **analysis** of the test coverage.

CONTENT AND PRESENTATION ELEMENTS	DESCRIPTION
ATE_COV.2.1C	The **analysis** of the test coverage shall **demonstrate** the correspondence between the tests in the test documentation and the TSFIs in the functional specification.
ATE_COV.2.2C	**The analysis of the test coverage shall demonstrate that all TSFIs in the functional specification have been tested.**

ATE_DPT.1 Testing: basic design

DEVELOPER ACTION ELEMENT	DESCRIPTION
ATE_DPT.1.1D	**The developer shall provide the analysis of the depth of testing.**
CONTENT AND PRESENTATION ELEMENTS	DESCRIPTION
ATE_DPT.1.1C	**The analysis of the depth of testing shall demonstrate the correspondence between the tests in the test documentation and the TSF subsystems in the TOE design.**
ATE_DPT.1.2C	**The analysis of the depth of testing shall demonstrate that all TSF subsystems in the TOE design have been tested.**

ATE_FUN.1 Functional testing

DEVELOPER ACTION ELEMENT	DESCRIPTION
ATE_FUN.1.1D	The developer shall test the TSF and document the results.
CONTENT AND PRESENTATION ELEMENTS	DESCRIPTION
ATE_FUN.1.2D	The developer shall provide test documentation.

ATE_IND.2 Independent testing - sample

DEVELOPER ACTION ELEMENT	DESCRIPTION
ATE_IND.2.1D	The developer shall provide the TOE for testing.
CONTENT AND PRESENTATION ELEMENTS	DESCRIPTION
ATE_IND.2.1C	The TOE shall be suitable for testing.
ATE_IND.2.2C	The developer shall provide an equivalent set of resources to those that were used in the developer's functional testing of the TSF.

The major difference between the Test Plan for EAL2 and EAL4 is that EAL4 requires that all of the TOE Security Functional Interfaces (TSFI) and all of the TOE subsystems are tested.

Note that the ATE_IND.2 (for both EAL2 and EAL4) requirements are satisfied by providing the TOE to the evaluators. There are no documentation requirements for this although the evaluators will use the Test Plan document to guide their independent testing. Evaluators will also re-run the tests performed by the developer as part of their independent testing and validation of the developer test results.

Test Plan Layout

The Test Plan should be treated as an historical accounting of the tests performed by the developer to demonstrate the Security Functional Requirements (SFRs) that are claimed in the Security Target (ST). This is different from the test plans developed by many commercial product testing groups. Product Quality Assurance (QA) teams often create test plans and test procedures to provide high-level guidance to other QA testers who are familiar with the product and the test environment. A fair amount of judgment and leeway is afforded the QA tester to perform their duties. However, because evaluators generally lack familiarity with the product and test environment, the Test Plan needs to provide greater detail and background information than test plans used by QA teams.

The primary audience for the Test Plan document is the evaluator. They will evaluate the test steps and test results provided by the developer but more importantly they will use it as a cookbook for their independent testing (ATE_IND.2).

The approach I advocate for creating the Test Plan is to assume that the evaluator knows very little about the product and technology. They may not know how to operate the product and they probably do not know how to install and configure it. The Test Plan document should be treated as a standalone guide for the evaluator to be able to replicate the test environment and test steps used by the developer. They expect that if they follow all of the steps in the Test Plan that they will obtain the (exact) same results that the developer did. Toward that end, the Test Plan document can be organized as follows.

1. Setting up the Test Environment
2. Installing the TOE
3. Test Cases
4. Test Coverage Summary

Setting Up the Test Environment

The evaluator will need all of the details for the prerequisite hardware, software, and networking used in the test environment. This will include the platforms for the TOE and any other systems used in performing the tests. Diagrams are helpful in illustrating the systems used in the test environment. An example is shown below.

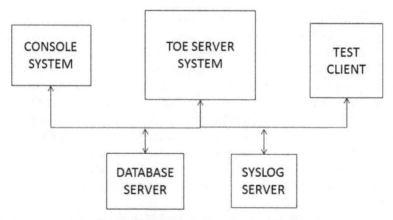

Figure 22 - Example Test Environment

182

The instructions for setting up the test environment can leverage the information from the Guidance document and the product installation guides but the specific details of the test environment used by the developer must be included. Details such as those shown in the following tables should be included in the Test Environment section of the Test Plan.

Note that the hardware and software used in the test environment must be consistent with the supported platform information provided in the Security Target.

TEST SYSTEM	REQUIREMENTS
TOE Server System	Dell PowerEdge T360 with Intel Xeon E5-2620 2GHz 6C/12T 8GB (2x4GB) 2 x 300GB 10K RPM Red Hat Linux Server 6.5 Java 1.7 IP Address: 192.100.20.1
Console System	HP Pavilion with AMD A8-Series - 8GB Memory - 2TB Hard Drive Microsoft Windows 7 Mozilla Firefox 11.0 IP Address: 192.100.20.2
Test Client System	HP Pavilion with AMD A8-Series - 8GB Memory - 2TB Hard Drive Microsoft Windows 7 Wireshark 1.6.5 WinPcap 4.1.2 Network traffic files provided by developer IP Address: 192.100.20.3
Database Server System	Dell PowerEdge T360 with Intel Xeon E5-2620 2GHz 6C/12T 8GB (2x4GB) 2 x 300GB 10K RPM Red Hat Linux Server 6.5 Oracle DBMS 11.0 IP Address: 192.100.20.4
Syslog Server System	Dell PowerEdge T360 with Intel Xeon E5-2620 2GHz 6C/12T 8GB (2x4GB) 2 x 300GB 10K RPM Red Hat Linux Server 6.5 including syslog IP Address: 192.100.20.5

Installing the TOE

The next section of the Test Plan includes instructions on how to properly install and configure the TOE for the test environment. These instructions should be identical to those given in the Guidance document. If there are any deviations to the Guidance document instructions, those should be noted and explained.

As in the Guidance document, there should be instructions on how to verify the complete and correct installation of the proper TOE (version).

Test Cases

The test cases are detailed instructions for the evaluator that demonstrate that the TOE meets all of the claimed SFRs. I suggest that test cases be broken down into relatively short tests that focus on a simple test objective. Creating tests that are long and complex can cause confusion and make it less clear as to how the security functions are implemented. Each test case should contain the following information and illustrated in the example below.

- Test Case Identifier
- Purpose
- SFR Coverage
- TSFI Coverage
- Prerequisites
- Test Steps
- Expected and Actual Results

Test Case 01

Purpose: Test administrator successful and unsuccessful login attempts. Show that appropriate log entries are made. Demonstrate that unsuccessful login attempts result in denying access to the TOE functions.

SFR Coverage:
FAU_GEN.1
FIA_UAU.1
FIA_UID.1

TSFI Coverage:
Admin Console Interface

184

Prerequisites:
Administrator user account has been created with user name= "admin" and password = "pwadmin"

Test Steps:
1. On the Console System, open the web browser and enter the IP address for the TOE Server (192.100.20.1). This will bring up the TOE login page.
2. Enter valid administrator user login credentials:
   a. User name = "admin"
   b. Password = "pwadmin"
3. Navigate to Auditing > View System Log
4. See Expected Result #1
5. Click the Sign Out button to log out of the TOE.
6. Enter invalid administrator user login credentials:
7. User name = "adminX"
8. Password = "pwadmin"
9. See Expected Result #2
10. Re-enter valid administrator user login credentials:
11. User name = "admin"
12. Password = "pwadmin"
13. Navigate to Auditing > View System Log
14. See Expected Result #3

Expected Results:
Expected Result #1 – System log entry shows successful login event.
Expected Result #2 – User is unable to access any TOE functions.
Expected Result #3 – System log entry shows unsuccessful login event.

Actual Results:
Actual Result #1
Audit log shows the successful login event entry.

```
2014-07-03 10:23:20 – User admin login attempt – successful
IP = 192.100.20.2
```

Actual Result #2
The user is unable to access any TOE functions.

Actual Result #3

185

Audit log shows the failed login event entry.

```
2014-07-03 10:23:20 – User admin login attempt – successful
IP = 192.100.20.2
2014-07-03 10:24:23  – User admin login attempt – failed
IP = 192.100.20.2
```

The example test case shows all of the necessary information for the evaluator to replicate the test and to see the results that the developer expected and obtained. These results will be checked against the results the evaluator obtains when they re-run the tests.

At EAL2, the test coverage requirement is merely to document what TOE Security Functional Interfaces (TSFI) were tested. Any TSFI that the developer does not test will be tested by the evaluator during their independent testing phase.

At EAL4, the developer must test all of the TSFI. This usually means that all of the "options" within the interface that demonstrate all of the aspects of the Security Functional Requirements (SFRs) must be tested. For example, FMT_MTD.1 Management of TSF data allows the developer to choose various management functions, TSF data, and user roles the TOE may support. At EAL4, all of these options will need to be tested and documented by the developer as shown in the example below.

FMT_MTD.1 Management of TSF data

FMT_MTD.1.1   The TSF shall restrict the ability to change default, query, modify, delete, clear, and no other operations the network protocol parameters, cryptographic algorithm parameters to system administrator, device administrator.

If the TOE claims it shall restrict the ability to change the default, query, modify, delete, and clear network protocol and cryptographic algorithm parameters to system administrator and device administrator roles, for EAL4, there should be test cases covering the following test matrix.

186

TEST CASE	DESCRIPTION
Test Case 01	Demonstrate that the System Administrator can change the default, query, modify, delete, and clear network protocol parameters and that appropriate audit log entries are made.
Test Case 02	Demonstrate that the System Administrator can change the default, query, modify, delete, and clear cryptographic algorithms parameters and that appropriate audit log entries are made.
Test Case 03	Demonstrate that the Device Administrator can change the default, query, modify, delete, and clear network protocol parameters and that appropriate audit log entries are made.
Test Case 04	Demonstrate that the Device Administrator can change the default, query, modify, delete, and clear cryptographic algorithms parameters and that appropriate audit log entries are made.

Note that these tests also cover parts of FAU_GEN.1 Audit data generation to obviate the need for separate tests to cover FAU_GEN.1 requirements. For EAL4, all of the audit events claimed in FAU_GEN.1 must be tested.

Test Coverage Summary

As a convenience for the evaluator and to make sure the test cases have the necessary coverage, the Test Coverage Summary section of the Test Plan is included. The summary is most easily presented using tables developed from the information provided in each test case description. The 3 test coverage matrices are the following with examples shown in the following pages.

1. Test Case vs. TSFI coverage
2. Test Case vs. SFR coverage
3. Test Case vs. Subsystem coverage

TSFI	TEST CASE
Console Interface	Test Case 01
	Test Case 02
	Test Case 03
Network Interface	Test Case 04
Database Interface	Test Case 03

Figure 23 - Test Case vs. TSFI Coverage

SFR	TEST CASE
FAU_GEN.1	Test Case 01
	Test Case 02
	Test Case 03
FIA_UAU_1	Test Case 01
FIA_UID.1	Test Case 01
FDP_ACC.1	Test Case 02
FDP_ACF.1	Test Case 02
FMT_MTD.1	Test Case 03
FMT_MSA.1	Test Case 03
FMT_MSA.3	Test Case 03
FMT_SMF.1	Test Case 03
FMT_SMR.1	Test Case 03
FTP_TRP.1	Test Case 04

Figure 24 - Test Case vs. SFR Coverage

SUBSYSTEM	TEST CASE
Audit Subsystem	Test Case 01
	Test Case 02
	Test Case 03
Management Subsystem	Test Case 02
	Test Case 03
Communications Subsystem	Test Case 04

Figure 25 - Test Case vs. Subsystem Coverage (EAL4)

TSFIs described in the Functional Specifications (FSP) document must be tested to meet the Test assurance requirements for both EAL2 (ATE_COV.1.1C) and EAL4 (ATE_COV.2.1C). For EAL2, the requirement is to just identify which TSFI were tested. For EAL4, all TSFI must be tested. Most developers opt to test all TSFI even at EAL2 just to make sure that all of the functionality is tested before the evaluators do their independent testing.

188

There is no explicit requirement to provide the mapping between test cases and Security Functional Requirements (SFRs) however all evaluators I've encountered expect this information to be provided for each test case. This implicit requirement probably stems from the requirement to test the TSFIs since they are a reflection of the SFRs. The Test Case vs. SFR summary table provides a quick reference to show that all of the functionality is covered.

At EAL4, ATE_DPT.1 requires that the test plan demonstrate that all subsystems in the TOE design have been tested. This table can be generated using the Modular Design (TDS) document's descriptions of the TOE subsystems and the interactions between them to perform the security functions. The test cases may be organized by testing the "functional threads" described in the TDS. These "functional threads" will show what subsystems (and modules) are invoked to perform the security functions. These subsystems are to be listed in the Test Case vs. Subsystem table.

Independent Testing

Independent testing is the testing performed by the evaluator to supplement the developer's tests. There are no additional documentation requirements for independent testing.

Generally, evaluators will evaluate the Test Plan document to gain enough understanding about how to set up the test environment and the developer test cases. From there, the evaluator will re-run some or all of the developer tests. They will then develop and execute their own set of tests to supplement the developer test cases.

The evaluator's goal during this phase is to ensure that the Test Plan instructions are clear, complete and accurate; that the test results are reproducible; and that all of the claimed functionality has been tested (either by the developer or evaluator).

There may be some functionality that cannot be tested directly or using readily available tools. For example, FDP_RIP.1 Subset residual information protection is often claimed by firewall and router TOEs to ensure against data leakage across user sessions by claiming that user buffers are overwritten before reuse. It is often difficult to test this action with assurance that the buffers are actually overwritten. This SFR may be verified through the evaluation of the Implementation Representation (i.e., source code review) rather than by direct testing. Arrangements can be made with the evaluator to handle this situation.

189

Chapter 21: Vulnerability Analysis

While CC evaluations focus on deriving assurance through assessment and not improving product security, the vulnerability analysis portion of the evaluation comes the closest to trying to improve the security of products. Not providing timely patches to mitigate security vulnerabilities is an on-going issue with commercial software products. Other priorities, constrained resources, and release timing interfere sometimes with the ability to deliver corrections to known security defects (vulnerabilities). Nonetheless, evaluators will not allow a CC evaluation to complete when there are known vulnerabilities in the TOE. Any open vulnerability must be addressed.

The requirement for EAL2 is AVA_VAN.2 Vulnerability analysis while the EAL4 requirement is AVA_VAN.3 Focused vulnerability analysis. Both content and presentation element requirements are the same but the difference is in the evaluator action elements. The developer requirements for AVA_VAN.2 are shown below.

AVA_VAN.2 Vulnerability analysis

DEVELOPER ACTION ELEMENT	DESCRIPTION
AVA_VAN.2.1D	The developer shall provide the TOE for testing.
CONTENT AND PRESENTATION ELEMENTS	DESCRIPTION
AVA_VAN.2.1C	The TOE shall be suitable for testing.

For EAL2, the evaluator shall perform a vulnerability analysis of the TOE using the CC documentation and other readily available resources to identify potential vulnerabilities in the TOE. They will scan the public vulnerability databases to look for known vulnerabilities that may impact the TOE and then perform basic penetration tests to verify the vulnerability exists in the TOE.

While there are no explicit developer documentation requirements for vulnerability analysis, evaluators commonly ask for a list of third-party and open source components that are included in the TOE. Open source vulnerabilities are the bane of CC evaluations. I've been involved in many evaluations which were delayed because the product team had to patch the TOE software to mitigate a newly-disclosed vulnerability in an open source component used by the TOE.

The list of third-party software used in the TOE should provide all of the component details including the specific version. Many evaluators use vulnerability scanner such as Nessus or Qualys to check for vulnerabilities as part of their penetration testing. These tools can be "noisy" or produce a lot of false positive results. It becomes the developer's responsibility to explain away these false positives. Oftentimes, while a component may have a known vulnerability, the TOE may not use the affected function in the component and thus the TOE is not vulnerable. To avoid unpleasant delays in the vulnerability analysis, it would be good for the developer to run these vulnerability scanners before the evaluator does.

The vulnerability analysis conducted by the evaluators for EAL4 is more focused and will include examination of the implementation representation (e.g., source code) and a more aggressive penetration testing regime. The [CEM] Appendix B goes into great detail about how evaluators should conduct vulnerability analyses.

PART VII: CONCLUSION

This part contains:
Chapter 22: Closing Remarks
References
Abbreviations

Chapter 22:   Closing Remarks

The need to produce the extensive set of documentation for Common Criteria (CC) evaluations is dwindling due to the adoption of the "NDPP Paradigm" by many national CC Schemes. The NDPP or Network Device Protection Profile is the first in a new generation of protection profiles (PPs) produced by the United States' National Information Assurance Partnership (NIAP). These protection profiles are set at EAL1 along with some other assurance requirements built into the PP. The documentation requirements for these evaluations are minimal. Until the adoption of this new paradigm is complete across all Schemes, there is a need for developers to produce the set of documentation I've described in this book.

I wanted to capture some of my CC documentation writing experiences and pass them along to those developers who are faced with either writing the documents themselves or hiring someone to do it for them. The CC evaluation process is still quite subjective in spite of the CC standards and the Common Evaluation Methodology (CEM). Evaluator experience, knowledge and skills are still important factors to consider when writing documentation that they will assess. Their interpretation of what you write will determine the success or failure of the CC evaluation. My hope is that this book helps ease the mechanics of creating these documents.

References

[CC1}   *Common Criteria for Information Technology Security
             Evaluation, Part 1: Introduction and general model,*
             September 2012. Version 3.1 Revision 4

[CC2}   *Common Criteria for Information Technology Security
             Evaluation, Part 2: Security functional components,*
             September 2012. Version 3.1 Revision 4

[CC3}   *Common Criteria for Information Technology Security
             Evaluation, Part 3: Security assurance components,*
             September 2012. Version 3.1 Revision 4

[CEM]   *Common Criteria for Information Technology Security
             Evaluation, Common Evaluation Methodology,*
             September 2012. Version 3.1 Revision 4

[Higaki]   Higaki, Wesley Hisao, *Successful Common Criteria
             Evaluations: A Practical Guide for Vendors,* July 21,
             2010

[Portal]   www.commoncriteriaportal.org

Abbreviations and Terms

AES	Advanced Encryption Standard
API	Application Programmatic Interface
CC	Common Criteria
CEM	Common Evaluation Methodology
CCTL	Common Criteria Testing Laboratory
CI	Configuration Item
CM	Configuration Management
CMVP	Cryptographic Module Validation Program
DB	Database
DVD	Digital Versatile Disc
EAL	Evaluation Assurance Level
EOR	Evaluation Observation Report
FIPS 140-2	Federal Information Processing Standard 140-2
GB	Gigabyte
GPC	General Purpose Computer
HMAC	Hashed Message Authentication Code
HTTPS	Hypertext Transfer Protocol Secure
IC	Integrated Circuit
I/F	Interface
IP	Internet Protocol
IP	Intellectual Property
IR	Implementation Representation
IT	Information Technology
LED	Light-Emitting Diode
MD5	Message Digest 5
NDPP	Network Device Protection Profile
NIAP	National Information Assurance Partnership
NIST	National Institute of Science and Technology
NTP	Network Time Protocol
OSP	Organizational Security Policy
PCB	Printed Circuit Board
PP	Protection Profile
QA	Quality Assurance
RFC	Request for Comment
ROI	Return on Investment

RPM	Revolutions Per Minute
SAR	Security Assurance Requirement
SFC	Security Functional Class
SFP	Security Function Policy
SFR	Security Functional Requirement
SHA-1	Secure Hash Algorithm 1
SME	Subject Matter Expert
SPD	Security Problem Definition
SSL	Secure Socket Layer
ST	Security Target
TB	Terabyte
TOE	Target of Evaluation
TSF	TOE Security Function
TSFI	TSF Interface
TSS	TOE Summary Specification
TTM	Time-to-Market
IU	User Interface
VPN	Virtual Private Network

Accreditation
Common Criteria (CC) testing and evaluation laboratories (CCTL) are accredited by national government agencies to conduct CC evaluations. Accreditation involves meeting quality process standards and demonstrated expertise in CC evaluations. FIPS 140 labs are also accredited using similar standards.

Architecture
Target of Evaluation (TOE) architecture refers to the high-level structure and design of the product including its major modules and interfaces. The Architecture may also include specific technologies used in the TOE.

Assurance
Assurance is confidence that the Target of Evaluation (TOE) or product will operate securely. Assurance is gained by independent, third-party evaluation against internationally-recognized security standards.

Augmentation
Security Assurance Requirements (SAR) contained in standard Evaluation Assurance Levels (EAL) may be augmented with additional SARs. For example, many products have been evaluated at EAL 4 augmented with ALC_FLR.2, Flaw Remediation. This adds the ALC_FLR.2 requirement to the standard set of SARs in EAL 4 to the evaluation.

Block Diagram
A product or Target of Evaluation (TOE) architecture can be depicted in a block diagram. The block diagram decomposes the TOE into its major modules and their interfaces.

Certification
Certification (or validation) marks the final, official completion of a successful Common Criteria evaluation. The national certificate-authorizing body certifies the results of the evaluation laboratory and issues a certificate to the sponsor (vendor).

Class, Family, Component, Element
Security Functional Requirements and Security Assurance Requirements are organized hierarchically into classes, families, components, and elements with each level defining greater specificity and details of each requirement.

Common Evaluation Methodology
The Common Evaluation Methodology (CEM) defines the requirements of the evaluator for CC evaluations. This standard along with supporting documents (SD) and protection profiles (PP) help ensure consistent evaluations around the world.

Configuration
Configuration refers to the settings or customization of products for use in customer environments. These configuration settings adjust for the unique deployment environment. Inappropriate security settings may result in exploitable vulnerabilities.

Configuration Management
Product configuration management (CM) controls and organizes the components of the product to ensure that all of the correct component versions are used to build the product. For software products, configuration management is usually managed by source code control tools such as CVS or Perforce.

Evaluation
Evaluation is the examination of evidence by independent, accredited third-party Common Criteria testing laboratories (CCTL). Independent examination against international standards is the foundation for the Common Criteria (CC). Security assurance is derived through evaluation.

Evaluation Assurance Level
The Evaluation Assurance Level (EAL) defines the depth of the evaluator examination. EALs are comprised of a set of Security Assurance Requirements (SAR). There are 7 EALs with EAL 1 being the least stringent and EAL 7 being the most stringent.

Evaluation Observation Report
Evaluators generate Evaluation Observation Reports (EOR) to record issues or comments they observe during the evaluation of evidence. EORs may note discrepancies or incomplete information in evidence documents. Vendors are expected to respond to EORs in order for the evaluation to continue.

Evaluation Test Report
The Evaluation Test Reports (ETR) are written by the evaluation lab recording their findings during their evaluation. Evaluation labs will generate interim ETRs as well as a final ETR that are reviewed by the validators or certifiers.

Extended Components
Customized Security Functional Requirements (SFR) or Security Assurance Requirements (SAR) may be developed if the standard

SFRs or SARs as defined in Common Criteria Parts 2 and 3 (respectively) do not apply to the Target of Evaluation (TOE).

External Interfaces
An external interface is a TOE interface to an external entity that plays a part in a security function. It is also known as a TOE Security Function Interface (TSFI)

Federal Information Processing Standard 140
Federal Information Processing Standard 140 (FIPS 140) is the standard maintained by the U.S. National Institute of Standards and Technology (NIST) and the Canadian Communications Security Establishment (CSE) pertaining to cryptographic module standards.

Flaw Remediation
Flaw Remediation is more commonly known as bug fixing. Flaw remediation refers to the entire process of reporting defects, developing patches or fixes, deploying the patches to affected systems, and advising customers.

Functional Specification
Functional Specification (FSP) documents describe the functions of the product or Target of Evaluation (TOE). The FSP provides a high-level description of what capabilities the product provides.

Implementation Representation
In software terms, Implementation Representation is the source code. Fro hardware, it may be the hardware diagrams.

In Evaluation
There is no internationally recognized definition for In Evaluation but generally speaking when a Security Target has been approved for evaluation, the validation Scheme will recognize the Target of Evaluation (TOE) as being In Evaluation status.

Internal Interface

An internal interface is a connection between TOE components, subsystems, or modules to perform security functions.

Interpretations

The Common Criteria (CC) standards were designed to be quite flexible and as such are subject to interpretation by national Schemes in order to meet local requirements and regulations. Each national Scheme is responsible for managing interpretations for use by evaluators and validators.

Platforms

Platforms refer to the computing base upon which application software will execute. The Platform may be viewed as the dependencies of the application software including: operating system, computer hardware and networking.

Protection Profile

Protection Profiles (PP) are documents intended to reflect customer security requirements for a particular technology type. PPs contain security functional requirements (SFR) and security assurance requirements (SAR) or Evaluation Assurance Level (EAL). Targets of Evaluation (TOE) may evaluate against the requirements within a PP and claim compliance to the PP by meeting all of the evaluation requirements in the PP.

Quality Assurance

Quality Assurance (QA) is a function within the developer organization chartered with the responsibility for establishing and executing product quality practices. The QA team is usually responsible for developing and executing product tests.

Rework

Rework refers to the editing and re-examination of Common Criteria (CC) evaluation evidence due to errors or omissions in the original evidence. Evidence documents are submitted to evaluators for their review and judgment. Should the evidence fail to meet the requirements of the evaluation, evaluators will return the evidence to the authors with comments in the form of Observation Reports (OR). The evidence authors are expected to rework the evidence and re-submit the revision for re-evaluation.

Scheme
Each member nation of the Common Criteria Mutual Recognition Agreement (CCRA) has a governing body or Scheme. The Scheme is responsible for representing that nation's interests in the Common Criteria (CC). The Scheme manages the validators.

Security Assurance Requirement
Security Assurance Requirements (SAR) are defined in Common Criteria standard part 3. SARs define the product development, delivery and installation processes. SARs are conveniently organized into sets called Evaluation Assurance Levels (EAL).

Security Functional Requirement
Security Functional Requirements (SFR) are defined in Common Criteria standard part 2. SFRs define the product's security features. SFRs may be extended or customized if the standard SFRs do not fit the Target of Evaluation.

Security Target
The Security Target (ST) is the foundational document of the Common Criteria (CC) evaluation. The ST defines what will be evaluated and to what depth. The ST contains all of the security claims for the Target of Evaluation (TOE). All subsequent evidence must be consistent with the ST claims.

Site Visit
Evaluators are required to conduct first-hand examinations of certain tools and procedures used by vendors during their development processes. Evaluators conduct these first-hand examinations during vendor development site visits.

Time-to-Market
Time-to-Market (TTM) is the concept that products that are introduced into the marketplace ahead of the competition enjoy a

revenue generation advantage. TTM drives product vendors to try to be first on the market with a new product or new capability.

TOE Boundary
The Target of Evaluation (TOE) Boundary sets the physical and logical limits of the evaluation. The TOE Boundary is defined in the Security Target (ST) document to advise evaluators and consumers what is included in the evaluation.

TOE Security Functionality
The Target of Evaluation Security Functionality (TSF) is the total security capability claimed by the Target of Evaluation (TOE). The TSF must meet the requirements of all of the claimed Security Functional Requirements (SFR) in the Security Target (ST) document.

Validation
Validation (or certification) is the final, official completion of a successful Common Criteria evaluation. The national certificate-authorizing body certifies the results of the evaluation laboratory and issues a certificate to the sponsor (vendor). The United States tends to use the term validation over certification.

Version
A Version is a uniquely identifiable variation or revision of a product. Common Criteria evaluations are valid only for a specified version of a product. That version is specified in the Security Target document.

Vulnerabilities
Vulnerabilities are security flaws or weaknesses that may be accidentally or maliciously exploited to expose unauthorized access to data or systems.

APPENDIX A: MODULAR DESIGN

EXAMPLE

In Chapter 17: Modular Design (EAL4), I presented a technique I use to create the TOE Design (TDS) document for EAL4, called Modular Design. This technique involves tracing through product functions that demonstrate the claimed security functional requirements (SFRs). This tracing through the "functional threads" results in gathering the information necessary to meet the documentation requirements for the Modular Design. In this appendix, I provide an example of this tracing exercise to illustrate how the module descriptions can be derived.

The example is the same as the configuration example described at the subsystem level in Chapter 16: Basic Design (EAL2) - Subsystem Description Creation Tip. It demonstrates an authorized user making changes to the system configuration or TOE Security Function (TSF) data which meets the FMT_MTD.1 – modifications to TSF data SFR. An audit record is generated when there are changes to the TSF data in accordance with FAU_GEN.1 – security audit generation. The following figure illustrates the subsystem level decomposition of the interfaces and interactions for this example.

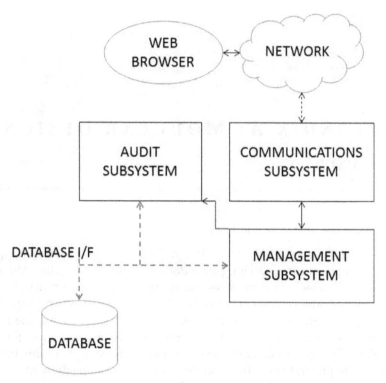

Figure 26 - Configuration Example - Subsystem Level

The next figure shows the example TOE decomposition at the modular level.

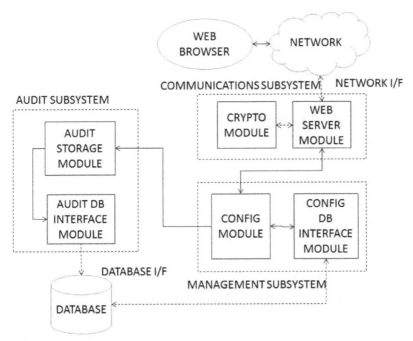

Figure 27 – Configuration Example - Module Level

In pseudo-code, here is the sequence of actions (i.e., "functional thread") at the module level.

Web Server Module
```
receive_HTTPS_input (user_info, in_buffer)
decrypt_input (in_buffer, decrypted_buffer)
Parse input buffer and if the action is to change
configuration then send_buffer_to_config (decrypt-
ed_buffer)
```

Config Module
```
receive_config_command (cfg_buffer)
Parse the input buffer and if the action is to change
configuration call retrieve_old_DB_record
(cfg_buffer, old_record)to ger current configuration
settings.
send_old_config_to_user (old_record)
```

Web Server Module
```
receive_config_data (config_record)
```

209

```
send_HTTPS_output(user_info, config_record)
receive_HTTPS_input (user_info, in_buffer)
decrypt_input (in_buffer, decrypted_buffer)
Parse input buffer and get the configuration changes
and then send_buffer_to_config (decrypted_buffer)
```

Config Module
```
receive_config_command (cfg_buffer)
Parse input buffer and get the configuration changes
then write_new_DB_record (new_config_buffer)
Create an audit event record using the old and new
configuration data and send_audit_event
(CONFIG_CHANGE, audit_data)
```

Audit Storage Module
```
receive_audit_event (event_type, audit_buffer)
write_audit_record (event_type, audit_buffer,
DB_error)
```

Given the above "functional thread" information, the description of the Config Module would include the following. Note that the complete module description would include information from other "functional threads" such as Policy Management and User Account Management.

Config Module Description

Purpose:
The Config Module is responsible for receiving changes to configuration settings from the user, writing those changes to the database and reporting the configuration change as an audit event.

Security Functionality:
The Config Module provides the following coverage of security functionality for changes to the configuration settings.

SFR	FUNCTIONALITY
FMT_MTD.1 (enforcing)	The Config Module allows only authorized users to modify, delete, add, and review the configuration settings for the TOE.

210

SFR	FUNCTIONALITY
FAU_GEN.1 (enforcing)	The Config Module sends a security event to the Audit Module when changes to the configuration data are made.

Module Interfaces

The Config Module exposes the following interfaces (APIs) to other modules.

INTERFACE	
API `send_buffer_to_config (decrypted_buffer)`	
PURPOSE Sends user commands to the Config Module for processing.	
PARAMETER	**PARAMETER DESCRIPTION**
decrypted_buffer	User commands
RETURN VALUES N/A	
CALLED BY SUBSYSTEM	**MODULE**
Communications Subsystem	Web Server Module

Module Interactions

The diagram below shows the interactions between the Config Module and other TOE subsystems and modules.

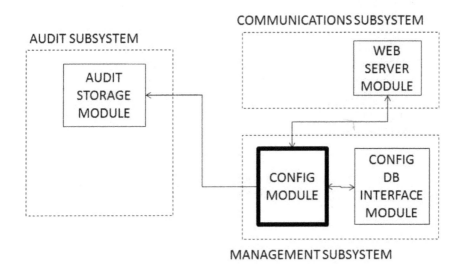

The table below summarizes the Config Module interactions.

SUBSYSTEM - MODULE	INTERFACE	ACTION
Communications Subsystem – Web Server Module	receive_config_command	Receive commands from the Web Server.
	send_old_config_to_user	Send current configuration settings to the Web Server module.
Management Subsystem – Config DB Interface Module	write_new_DB_record	Sends the new configuration settings to the database.
Audit Subsystem – Audit Storage Module	send_audit_event	Sends audit event to audit log.

Configuration Changes Functional Thread
The Config Module receives a command from the Web Server Module by calling the following function.

INTERFACE
PROVIDER
Communications Subsystem – Web Server Module
API
`receive_config_command (cfg_buffer)`
PURPOSE
Receive configuration command from the web server module. This command originalted from the user.

PARAMETER	PARAMETER DESCRIPTION
cfg_buffer	Configuration buffer

RETURN VALUES
N/A

The Config Module parses the command to change a configuration and retrieves the current configuration settings from the Config DB Interface Module.

INTERFACE
PROVIDER
Management Subsystem – Config DB Interface Module
API
`retrieve_old_DB_record (cfg_buffer, old_record)`
PURPOSE
Retrieve the configuration settings from the database.

PARAMETER	PARAMETER DESCRIPTION
cfg_buffer	Configuration settings request

RETURN VALUES
old_record = Current configuration settings

The Config Module sends the current configuration settings to the Web Server Module.

INTERFACE
PROVIDER
Communications Subsystem – Web Server Module
API
`send_old_config_to_user (old_record)`
PURPOSE
Send current configuration settings to the Web Server module. This data will be presented to the user to make changes.

PARAMETER	PARAMETER DESCRIPTION
old_record	Current configuration settings

RETURN VALUES
N/A

The Config Module retrieves the configuration changes from the Web Server Module using the following function call.

INTERFACE
PROVIDER
Communications Subsystem – Web Server Module
API
`receive_config_command (cfg_buffer)`
PURPOSE
Receive configuration command from the web server module. This command originalted from the user.

PARAMETER	PARAMETER DESCRIPTION
cfg_buffer	Configuration buffer

INTERFACE
RETURN VALUES
N/A

The Config Module parses the configuration command and configuration changes and sends them to the Config DB Interface Module.

INTERFACE	
PROVIDER	
Management Subsystem – Config DB Interface Module	
API	
`write_new_DB_record (new_config_buffer)`	
PURPOSE	
Sends the new configuration settings to the database.	
PARAMETER	**PARAMETER DESCRIPTION**
new_config_buffer	New configuration settings
RETURN VALUES	
N/A	

The Config Module then creates the audit event record and sends it to the Audit Storage Module in the Audit Subsystem.

INTERFACE	
PROVIDER	
Audit Subsystem – Audit Storage Module	
API	
`send_audit_event (event_type, audit_data)`	
PURPOSE	
Send audit event record to audit storage module.	
PARAMETER	**PARAMETER DESCRIPTION**
event_type	CONFIG_CHANGE = configuration change audit event.
audit_data	Modifications to configuration settings. Includes date , time, module identifier, successful transaction flag, changes made to the configuration settings.
RETURN VALUES	
N/A	

INDEX

215

Application programmatic
  interface – see API
Application software, 46, 49, 59,
  13, 141
Architecture
  security, 18, 22-23, 26, 46,
    86, 125-126, 130-136
  TOE, 130
ASE – see Security Target
Asset, 51, 53, 67-68
Assignment operation in SFR,
  39-41, 43, 54, 79
Assurance, derived through
  examination, 21
Assurance class, 21-22
Assurance family, 21
Assumption
  in Security Target, 51-54, 67-
    75, 83
  preparative procedures, 173-
    174
  security architecture, 132, 135
  site visit, 120
  system clock, 38, 46
Attacks, 35, 37, 72
ATE, 22-23, 28, 48, 86-88, 178-
  189
AVA, 22-23, 86-87, 166, 190-
  191
Audit
  event, 38, 141, 147, 162-163,
    187, 208-212
  log, 35, 39-40, 84, 89-90, 141,
    151-153, 175, 185-187
  record, 38-39, 46, 61, 89, 103,
    151-153, 176, 207
  record filtering, 38
  review, 37, 39, 132, 152
  storage, 39, 151-152, 158,
    163, 208-212
  subsystem, 132, 146-154,
    158-163, 188, 207-214
Augmented EAL, 18, 24
Authentication message – see
  HMAC

B

Badge, visitor, 114
Basic design, 18, 22-23, 86-87,
  131, 145-154
Bill-of-materials, 99
Binary code, 57, 98, 104
Black box, 126, 128, 137
Boot-up, 134-135
Boundary, TOE – see TOE
  Boundary
Bug – see flaw
Bugzilla, 104,115
Build, 57, 94, 98, 106

C

Certificate,
  CC, 35, 37
  key, 135
Checksum, 106, 143, 175
Code,
  binary – see binary code
  design language, 127, 166
  pseudo-, 207
  review, 61, 120, 127, 189
  source – see source code
  walk-through, 160
Comment-and-response, 20
Commercial product
  applicable SFRs, 36-47, 67
  delivery process, 107
  developers, 17, 24
  evaluation, 17, 19, 33-34, 48-
    50
  flaw remediation, 95, 110, 116
  functional specifications, 137,
    140
  installation instructions, 175
  modules, 160
  platform support, 174
  security measures, 113-114
  test plans, 181
  updates, 25
  vulnerabilities, 190
Common Criteria

216

Key, cryptographic – see
Cryptographic key

L

Language
 CC, 33, 56, 128
 plain, 128
 prose, 33, 56
LED, 139
Leverage, 79, 131, 183
Library, 160
Lifecycle model – see ALC_LCD
Limit
 access, 113-114
 number of platforms, 50
 rework cycles – see Rework
Linkage between SFRs, 161
Linux, 49, 60, 174, 183
Log, audit – see Audit log
Logical architecture of the TOE,
 131
Logical boundaries of the TOE,
 53
Logical decomposition of the
 TOE, 126, 146-147, 155
Logical scope of the TOE, 56,
 58, 61
Login, 42, 61, 89, 128, 132,
 141, 162, 184-186
Logistics, 120
Logout, 61, 89, 132

M

Maintenance, 94-96, 109-110
Management
 configuration - see Configuration Management
 functions, 78, 84, 134, 186
 policy – see Policy, management
 security – see Security, management
 subsystem, 150, 152, 163,
 188, 212-214
Mapping

dependency, 85
implementation representa-
 tion, 127, 157, 166-167
objectives, 71, 74, 83-84
product functions to SFR, 43,
 56
subsystem-to-SFR, 154
TDS, 155-156
test cases, 160, 178, 187-189
TSFI, 143-146
Marketing, 48,
Malicious entity, 133-135
Message authentication – see
 HMAC
Method of use, 137-142
Microsoft
 Event Viewer, 39
 Internet Explorer, 61
 Visual Studio, 115
 Windows, 39, 49, 60, 160,
 183
 Word, 27
Middleware, 49-50
Miscommunications with
 evaluator, 30
Modification
 and disclosure, 135
 of TOE, 25, 50, 96, 102
 of behavior, 39, 46
 of configuration item, 95, 103
 of data, 132, 150, 152, 207,
 214
Module, cryptographic – see
 Cryptography, module
Module interaction – see
 Interaction, module
Module interface, 162-165
Modular design, 18, 23, 155-165
Mozilla
 Bugzilla – see Bugzilla
 Firefox – see Firefox

N

Naming
 consistency, 128

Permissive default values – see
Default values, permissive
and restrictive
Personnel
in flaw remediation, 118-119
objectives, 69-70, 73-75
security measures, 93-94,
112-114
Phase exit criteria, 110-111
Physical
architecture, 131-136
characteristics of the operational environment, 69-70,
73, 174
decomposition into subsystems, 146-147
development security
measures, 93-94, 112-114
interface, 139
module representations, 126,
155
separation of part of the TOE,
36
TOE boundaries, 53, 56-58
Plain language – see Language,
plain
Platform
supported, 49-50, 173-174,
183
TOE, 134, 174-175, 182
Policy
enforcement, 133, 135-136,
146-147, 152
management, 158-160, 164,
208
organizational security, 51,
53-55, 67-60, 73-75, 83
Printed circuit board – see PCB
Priority, 26, 118-119
Prioritization, 110, 118-119
Privilege, 21, 41-43, 84, 114,
135, 172, 176
Procedure, acceptance, 23, 86,
101, 109
Procedure, control, 109

Process, development, 17, 125
Procurement requirement, 19
Product
change, 50
commercial, - see Commer-
cial product
feature – see Feature, product
manuals – see Guidance,
product manuals and guides
release, 33, 57, 67, 110-111,
116-117, 190
type, 50
Production environment, 105
Project management
Protection Profile, 34, 50
demonstrable conformance –
see Conformance, to pro-
tection profile, demonstrable
gap analysis – see Gap analysis
network device protection
profile – see NDPP
strict conformance – see
Conformance, to protection
profile, strict conformance
Protocol – see Network,
protocol
Prototyping, 111
Purpose
interface, 126, 137-142, 163-
165
module, 156, 158, 161-162,
208-212
subsystem, 150-151, 158-159
test case, 184
tool, 115

Q

Quality, 116
control, 26
QA, 121, 181
Qualys, 192

R

Rationale

assurance requirements, 87
conformance, 63-66
dependency, 84-85
dependency on FPT_STM, 46
extended components, 76, 80
objectives, 53, 71-72, 74-75, 84
protection profile gap analysis, 50
security requirements, 80-81, 83-84
Reference, ST, 51, 55-56
Reference, TOE, 25, 51, 55, 57, 98
Refinement, SFR, 45, 54
Reproducible tests, 189
Resource
  allocated, 50
  commitment, 26
  constrained, 25, 190
  non-IT, 73
  protected, 44, 58, 136
  security domain, 133
  test environment, 179, 181
  threat, 68
Response to evaluator comments, 29-30, 90, 99
Responsibility
  In flaw remediation, 118
  in lifecycle, 109-110
  in vulnerability analysis, 192
  of individuals on configuration items, 103
  of Operational Environment to address Assumptions, 73
Restrictive default values – see Default values, permissive and restrictive
Results
  actual – see Actual results
  expected - see Expected results
Return-on-investment – see ROI
Review
  audit – see Audit, review

code –see Code, review
Revision control system – see source code control system
Rework, 27, 29-30, 90
RFC, 141-143
ROI, 25
Role, user – see User role
Roles and responsibilities – see Responsibility
RSA Access Manager – see EMC RSA Access Manager

S

Schedule, 50, 121
Schematics, 96
Scheme – see National Scheme
Scope, manage project, 25
Scope of evaluation, 28, 33, 35, 37, 51, 174-175
Scope, TOE, 35, 39, 48, 56, 58, 61, 73, 174
Screenshots, 103
Scrum, 111
Secure development, 28, 121
Secure Socket Layer – See SSL
Security
  assurance, 48, 52, 64, 77, 80, 85-87, 130
  domain, 125, 130-131, 133-134
  management, 36-37, 42-43, 62, 79, 132, 144, 148
  -related, 37, 48, 177
  -relevant, 33, 89, 137, 172
Security Functional Classes, 17, 36, 58, 61, 79-80, 88-89
Security Assurance Requirements – see Assurance Class, see also EAL
SFR
  -enforcing, 125-126, 130-131, 166
  -non-interfering, 126, 146, 156
  -related, 156
  -relevant, 150

CC document, 99
product and TOE, 25, 33, 57-58, 67, 98, 103, 105, 107, 175, 184
software – see Software, version
third-party software, 192
tool, 103, 114-115, 118, 121
Virtual appliance, 106
Virus – see Anti-virus
Visitors, 114
VPN, 40, 42, 106, 114
Vulnerability, 34, 37

analysis and search, 22-23, 67, 86-87, 166, 190--191
open source, 190-191
publicly-disclosed, 119

W

White box testing, 128
Wireshark, 183
WinPcap, 183
Workflow, defect handling, 118